Ruin and Restoration:
St Mary's Church, Haddington

Rosalind K Marshall

for
Clifford and Kathleen

Designed by
East Lothian Council
Printed by
D & J Croal Ltd
Published by
East Lothian Council Library Service

ISBN 1 897857 23 3
2001

East Lothian Council
LIBRARY SERVICE

Prelude

A ROUGH WOOING

In the summer of 1544 Edward Seymour, Earl of Hertford, stood on a hillside above Edinburgh and watched the smoke rise from the burning houses below. On his orders, his soldiers had set fire to the town, the Abbey of Holyrood was in flames and the wind brought to his ears the wailing of the women and the poor folk whose homes were being destroyed. He was well satisfied. A few days earlier he had landed near Leith at the head of an English army of invasion, carrying detailed instructions from Henry VIII. 'Put all to fire and the sword,' his King had commanded him, 'Burn Edinburgh town, so razed and defaced when you have sacked and gotten what you can of it as there may remain forever a perpetual memory of the vengeance of God lightened upon [the Scots] for their falsehood and disobedience.' He was to burn Edinburgh's port of Leith as well, 'putting man, woman and child to fire and sword, without exception, where any resistance shall be made against you.'

Henry VIII was furious with the Scots. As the allies of his great enemy, France, they had long posed a constant threat on his northern border and all his attempts to persuade his nephew, the Scottish King James V, to abandon the French had failed. He had tried everything. He had arranged for a search of England's ancient records in the vain hope of finding proof that he was overlord of Scotland, he had played with the notion of kidnapping James and in the end he had sent his army against him, defeating the Scots at Solway Moss in November 1542. Less than a month later, James was dead and his throne had passed to his six-day-old daughter, Mary, Queen of Scots. Henry immediately saw his opportunity. If the baby Queen were to marry his own son and heir, Prince Edward, then Scotland would be his. The Scots would not relish the prospect, of course, and the French Queen Mother, Mary of Guise would be against it, but with the threat of an English invasion there was little any of them could do. Henry soon browbeat the new Regent of Scotland, the diffident, irresolute James, 2nd Earl of Arran, into agreeing to the match and on 1 July 1543 Arran signed the Treaties of Greenwich. Immediately after her tenth birthday, the little Queen would be taken to London to marry Prince Edward.

Henry's triumph was short-lived. No sooner had Arran signed the treaties than he was assailed by dreadful doubts and his dilemma was not helped by constant warnings of disaster from Mary of Guise, from Scotland's Chancellor, Cardinal David Beaton, and from his own half-brother the Abbot of Paisley. Always at the mercy of a stronger personality, he changed his mind and on 11 December he and the Scottish parliament repudiated the agreement. The marriage of Mary, Queen of Scots and Prince Edward would not now take place. This, then, was the cause of Henry's fury. Determined that he was not going to be cheated of the ideal solution to his northern problem, he resolved to force the match through and sent Hertford north in what was to be the first of the series of devastating invasions of Scotland known as 'The Rough Wooing'.

Having set fire to Scotland's capital, Hertford decided against trying to take Edinburgh Castle, which was virtually impregnable, and instead he rode into Lothian, burning and looting as he went. He then crossed to St Andrews in Fife, where he followed Henry VIII's instructions that he should turn every building upside down so that 'the upper stone may be the nether, and not one stick stand by another, sparing no creature alive within the same.' That done, he sailed back across the River Forth and marched south, heading for the border. On the way, he set fire to Musselburgh, Preston, Seton Palace and the royal burgh of Haddington. The French sent assistance to the Scots the following June, but that September Somerset was back, burning crops in the fertile valley of the River Tweed and setting fire to the abbeys of Melrose, Jedburgh and Dryburgh before marching south once more.

The death of Henry VIII in January 1547 brought no respite, for his young son succeeded as Edward VI and the man chosen to rule England on his behalf was none other than the Earl of Hertford, soon to be Duke of Somerset. On 1 September 1547 Somerset invaded Scotland yet again and defeated Arran and the Scottish army at Pinkie, near Musselburgh on 10 September. 'Black Saturday', the chroniclers called it, declaring that the waters of the Esk Burn ran with blood for three days afterwards. Somerset's responsibilities as Lord Protector soon took him back to London, but while Mary of Guise sent urgent messages to her old friend King Henri II of France asking for further assistance, Somerset was busily planning his next move. In January 1548 he sent instructions to one of his commanders, William, 13th Lord Grey of Wilton, a native of Kent who had distinguished himself during the English campaigns in France in the early 1540s and had led the first charge against the Scots at Pinkie. Although dreadfully wounded in the mouth, Grey had survived to become Governor of Berwick and Warden of the Marches. Somerset now ordered him to march north and capture Haddington, setting up his headquarters either in the town's tolbooth or in the parish church of St Mary the Virgin.

Chapter 1

THE CHURCH OF ST MARY THE VIRGIN

Haddington stands on the River Tyne in East Lothian, seventeen miles east of Edinburgh and thirty-six miles north of Berwick-upon-Tweed. In the sixteenth century its ground plan resembled a long, triangular pouch, bounded on the north by Market Street and on the south by the High Street. Between them was the spacious market place, with its market cross. The High Street was the principal route into the town and wealthy merchants and tradesmen lived there, in handsome houses backing on to very long gardens. The tolbooth stood at the east end of Market Street, a sturdy building with a prison where local lawbreakers were detained. A narrow lane called Tolbooth Wynd ran east from there to meet Hardgate, which lay parallel to the river and led into Sidegate. The candlemakers, as was usual, were restricted to the quiet back lanes, for by the very nature of their business there was always the danger of fire breaking out in their premises.

On the south side of the town, close to the river stood the Parish Church of St Mary the Virgin with its graveyard. No one knows when the church was founded, but Haddington lay within the diocese of St Andrews and it is recorded that in 1139 David I granted St Mary's with its chapels, lands and rights to the recently established Priory of Augustinian Canons in St Andrews. Ever since then, while Haddington town council provided for the priests, the Prior of St Andrews had been responsible for the upkeep of the chancel. This was the part of the church containing the high altar and the area in front of it, which was lined with benches for the clergy and choristers. At St Mary's the term 'chancel' has been little used throughout the centuries, and instead people spoke of 'the choir', meaning the entire east end. In what follows, I have accordingly followed that practice.

A little to the north of the church, between Hardgate and the river, stood another ecclesiastical building, the thirteenth-century Franciscan Friary. It was known to the local people as 'The Lamp of Lothian', in part because the light streaming from its large, graceful windows on dark winter days made it a landmark, in part because the friars were spreading spiritual enlightenment by preaching to the community. Finally, across the medieval Nungate Bridge and about a mile away from the parish church was the important Cistercian nunnery founded in the twelfth century by Countess Ada of Huntingdon, mother of King William the Lion. It seems that King William frequently lived in Haddington and indeed his son, the future Alexander II, was born there, but no trace of any royal castle has been found.

Haddington was a prosperous community. A royal burgh since the time of David I, it exported wool, woollen cloth, fleeces and hides through its port of Aberlady on the estuary of the River Forth. Once a week people from the surrounding countryside brought in their grain, eggs, poultry, fruit and vegetables to be sold at the market. There were meal and fish markets too, over by the wall of the Franciscan Friary, and a salt market was held in Hardgate. However, situated as it was on the main route from the Borders to the Scottish capital, the town was strategically important and therefore vulnerable to attack. Whenever the English invaded, Haddington lay in their path. It had been burned by King John of England in 1216, King Henry III in 1241 and King Edward III in 1333. Edward sacked Haddington on market day, killing many of the traders and in 1356 the English had returned, setting fire to both the parish church and the friary. Lamenting the damage done to the friary, one chronicler remarked that 'the Lamp of the Lothians was the singular solace of the people of that place'.

After the destruction, the inhabitants of Haddington waited, as they always did, until the armies had departed and then they determinedly set about repairing their buildings. By 1356, the parish church had become too small for the growing population and the town council therefore decided that St Mary's should be rebuilt

The cross carved in about 1400 on one of the pillars, to mark the consecration of St Mary's. *(Duncan Brash)*

on a far grander scale. No record survives to tell us the name of the master mason who was employed as architect, but the new building was to be in the shape of a cross. Cartloads of red sandstone were dragged from nearby Garvald, yellowish-white sandstone was brought from Seggarsdean and work began.

The choir was erected first, on the site of the original church, and it was built mainly of the red sandstone. The transepts forming the arms of the cross came next, and then the nave, mostly of Seggarsdean stone. They were constructed on part of the graveyard. Last of all, above the crossing, where the choir, transepts and nave met, a three-storey tower was put up. Ninety feet high, it was probably surmounted by the type of crown steeple still seen today at St Giles in Edinburgh. Three bells were then hung in the bell-chamber at the top, each apparently bearing Haddington's crest of a goat standing on its hind legs, eating grapes from a vine.

The new Church of St Mary the Virgin was consecrated in about 1400. At 206 feet long and 62 feet wide, it was the largest parish church in Scotland. Designed in the Gothic style, the lofty interior rose to a vaulted ceiling, multi-coloured light filtering in through the tall, pointed, stained glass windows. Two rows of nine great pillars ran the length of the church, forming a north and south aisle at each side. Between the two pillars at the east end stood the high altar, a screen called a reredos behind it. Behind that was the sanctuary, the space between the back of the reredos and the east wall. Beneath the great east window was a small alcove where the bread and wine for the Mass were kept before being consecrated.

In front of the altar, choir stalls ran along the north and south walls, facing each other. Not all churches had music. Only the cathedrals and the great burgh churches could afford to employ choristers, but at Haddington there was a full choir and in the late 1530s the town council, agreeing to give the priest choristers financial support, laid down a set of rules for their duties and appointed a Master to make sure that these were strictly carried out. The council then asked David Beaton, Archbishop of St Andrews, to sanction the arrangement, which he did. This type of organisation was known as a college, and so St Mary's became a collegiate church.

The choir was separated from the nave by the rood screen, a carved wooden screen with a large cross above it. The nave was largely empty of furniture. Because there were few sermons, most churches had neither a pulpit nor fixed seating. There may have been one or two benches for elderly parishioners, but for the most part people stood or knelt in prayer and, if they meant to attend a lengthy service, they would bring their own seats with them. Even during Mass, St Mary's would not, however, have been a place of hushed and holy calm. Like all other medieval churches, it was the centre of the community and people came there not only to pray but for a variety of other reasons which had little to do with religion. Notaries conducted their business in the church, and so those who wished to engage in legal transactions came along, friends strolled about and gossiped, dogs barked and snarled, young men and women flirted with each other and there was a good deal of laughing and talking, even during services.

Each day, Mass was celebrated at the high altar. When the parishioners who were in the church heard the ringing of the sanctus bell, they knew that the service was about to begin and they crowded forward towards the rood screen. The choir beyond was the holiest part of the building and only the clergy and the choristers were allowed there, so the parishioners had to peer through the carving of the rood screen to see what was happening. If they had a poor view, they could at least hear the chanting and the Latin words of the priest, but it was very important for them to see if they possibly could. Originally, the Mass had been a simple service commemorating The Last Supper, when Christ had his final meal with His apostles, but over the centuries an elaborate ceremonial had grown up. The Church now taught that when the bread and wine were blessed by the priest, these elements were transformed literally into the body and the blood of Christ. The Mass had become not merely a commemoration but a re-enactment of Christ's sacrifice on the cross, a miracle charged with deep spiritual significance, and the choir was screened off from the rest of the church to intensify the air of mystery.

After the first part of the service the priest, facing the altar and with his back to the nave, lifted the bread high above his head, saying in Latin, 'This is my body'. At that moment, the climax of the Mass, the sanctus bell was rung again, extra candles on the altar were lit, priests swung censers, wafting incense through the choir, and those taking part clasped their hands in prayer. Everyone bowed to the Host, as the bread was called, and the parishioners beyond the screen fell to their knees. They believed that, even if they were not taking part in the service, the very sight of the consecrated Host would bring them important benefits. Bishop Thomas Brinton of Exeter had usefully listed these for his congregation in 1375. Once they had seen the bread, he explained, people would feel no need for food for some time afterwards. Their eyesight would not fade, they would not age in the immediate aftermath, sudden death would not strike them and angels would protect them at every step.

After he had consecrated the bread, the priest with a less dramatic gesture raised the chalice containing the wine, which he himself would drink. Parishioners did not receive the wine, for only the priest was allowed to have the blood of Christ, but they were given the bread, in the form of specially baked wheaten wafers, marked with a cross or with the letters I.H.S., an abbreviation of the Greek word for Jesus. Most people took Communion once a year only, usually at Easter, after going to confession and doing penance for their sins. The fact that they communicated so rarely was not seen as a sign of apathy. It was, rather, a token of the supreme importance of the Mass, and even those who had little interest in spiritual affairs believed in its profound effect.

Whether they attended as participants or spectators, whether they came out of conviction or merely from habit, people in the late Middle Ages were preoccupied with what was going to happen to them in the next world and they regarded the Mass as a valuable source of assistance. Life expectancy was short, warfare, plague and flood were all too frequent and death was a daily companion. The Church said that, when people died, their souls would go to purgatory to suffer for their sins before finally being allowed to enter heaven. Anxious to reduce their period of torment, men and women therefore endowed special Masses to be said for themselves and for dead relatives. They could also pay for Masses to be said for recovery from illness, for a good harvest, or even for curing sick

The scallop shell, badge of pilgrims to the shrine of St James of Compostella, Spain, carved at a height of eight feet on the pillar beside the west gallery. (*Duncan Brash*)

farm animals. Since Mass could be celebrated only once a day at any particular altar, not only did more and more priests have to be employed but the number of altars multiplied too.

In St Mary's there were seventeen altars as well as the high altar of the Virgin Mary. Most of these side altars were dedicated to saints: Scotland's patron saint, St Andrew; St Anne, the mother of the Virgin; St Aubert; St Eloi (Blaise); the apostle St James the Great; St John the Baptist; St John the Evangelist; St Catherine the Virgin; St Michael the Archangel and Saints Crispin and Crispian; St Nicholas; St Ninian; St Peter; Saints Severus and Bartholomew; and St Thomas. There were also altars of The Trinity, St Salvator, sometimes known as the altar of The Holy Blood, and the Three Kings of Cologne, so called because the skulls of the Three Wise Men are allegedly preserved in a jewel encrusted gold shrine in Cologne Cathedral. Occasionally the documents of the time mention the location of a particular altar, and so we know that the Trinity Altar stood in the west part of the south aisle, the altar of The Three Kings was in the north west chapel and the altar of St James was in the nave. St James was a favourite saint, and John of Haddington in 1411 and Tom of Kello in 1535 were just two of those who made the pilgrimage from Haddington to the shrine of St James at Compostella, in Spain. Indeed, one of the great pillars in St Mary's still bears a carving of the scallop shell which was the badge of St James and was worn in their hats by those who undertook the pilgrimage.

Parishioners who endowed Masses always specified at which altar these were to be celebrated. In July 1454, for example, a wealthy Haddington burgess named Robert of Ingaldistoun arranged that when he and his wife died, a chaplain would say Mass for their souls every Wednesday at the altar of St John the Baptist. Robert paid for this by promising twenty shillings a year from his property on the south side of Market Street. As well as taking care of their own souls, quite a few people included the monarch and other members of the Scottish royal family in their endowments. In 1480 Richard Carpenter of Harpendene arranged for Masses to be said at the high altar not only for himself, his parents and other relatives, but for the souls of James III, his Queen, Margaret of Denmark and their children and in 1521 William Kemp, who owned property in Sidegate, specified himself, his wife Janet Cockburn, James V, at that time eight years old, the Scottish Regent John, Duke of Albany and Robert, Bishop of Ross.

The wealthier the donor, the more elaborate the service tended to be. In 1494 Marion Lawson, the widow of John Lawson, a local burgess, chose to have Masses for the souls of her husband, her dead son and herself sung every year on St Mungo's Day, 14 January, at the altar of St Catherine the Virgin. Seven priests and the parish clerk of the choir were to sing the vespers and dirge of the office of the dead, and two chaplains would say the requiem. Masses with music always cost more, and Marion's payment included provision for the priest choristers, lights and bells. Richard Carpenter had asked for eight chaplains and a clerk, and William Kemp gave even more detail. Nine chaplains of the choir and clerks were to take part, with four other priests not from the choir and a bell-ringer. The chaplain was to wear vestments when he celebrated the Mass, and William paid for the priests' wine, the bread, candles and other necessities.

Wealthy individuals not only funded special services. They also provided the silver chalices and plates used at the Mass. John of Furde presented the altar of St Peter with a silver chalice weighing over 12 ounces on 28 May 1426 and in the early sixteenth century William Kemp gave the altar of St James the Apostle a silver chalice and plate. Both had the words 'Saint James' engraved on them, and round the foot of the chalice was the inscription, in Latin, 'Pray for William Kemp and his spouse', while the Trinity Altar silver double overgilt paten or plate bore not only the name of its donor, Mr Robert Wandestoun, but his coat of arms too.

A list made on 9 June 1545 notes that the chalice and paten belonging to the altar of St John the Baptist had been given into the keeping of William Cockburn. William Kemp's chalice and paten went to James Mauchlin, while Thomas Mauchlin was looking after the silver gilt chalice of the high altar. The Mauchlin family were, incidentally, well represented among the clergy of St Mary's: another Mauchlin, Patrick, had been the Rood chaplain until his death the previous June. It may be that the 1545 distribution of the plate was an emergency measure, and that the individual priests were being charged with the safekeeping of the silver because the latest English invasion was believed to be imminent. On the other hand, the ninth and final entry on the little list reads, 'The high altar chalice to be restored within 8 days' and so there may have been a less dramatic explanation. Perhaps it was simply that some cleaning or refurbishment of the church interior was taking place.

Individual parishioners were not alone in endowing Masses and giving plate. The local craftsmen were organised into various Trades Incorporations, and these organisations took responsibility for different altars, usually those with which they had a special connection. St Crispin and St Crispianus were the patron saints of shoemakers, and so in July 1531 the shoemakers of Haddington decided to pay for the upkeep of the altar of St Michael the Archangel, St Crispin and St Crispianus. The bakers looked after the altar of St Aubert, the smiths took care of the altar of their patron, St Eloi the apostle of Flanders and the tailors paid a penny a week to their altar of St Anne. When a boy was apprenticed to a tailor, he had to pay six shillings and eight pence to the altar and ten shillings when he was admitted to the incorporation.

In 1544, the provost, bailies and town council decided that the skinners and furriers should share the responsibility for St Anne's altar with the tailors. This arrangement probably came about after a lot of wrangling, for the various trades guarded their rights fiercely. Four years earlier, the maltmen who were responsible for St Andrew's altar had been complaining bitterly about others infringing their monopoly. There was often trouble, too, when craftsmen failed to make the required payments. On 4 February 1533, James Scheyle was ordered to pay a pound of wax to St Andrew's altar because he had not made his rightful contribution to its upkeep.

A few years before that there had been a fierce disagreement between the wrights and masons on the one part and the chaplain of the altar of St John the Baptist on the other. The wrights and masons had apparently been responsible for that altar, but they had gained permission to establish a new altar to St John the Evangelist and they had taken back some of the offerings they had promised to the St John the Baptist chaplain. The chaplain sued them and in the end they had not only to give back the money but they had to supply a new statue of a saint named Doicho (perhaps the Celtic St Duthac) for the St John the Baptist altar, as well as giving assurances that they would pay for the necessary candles, Mass-cloths and services for the new altar.

Finally, another dispute, unimportant as it seems, may have been significant. On 20 May 1537, Mungo Millar, one of the chaplains, knelt before the high altar at the time of Mass and begged the forgiveness of another chaplain, John Tait. He had accused Tait of saying that the Virgin Mary had no more power than any other woman to help mankind. This may have been merely a petty quarrel between colleagues, but in the early sixteenth century there was growing criticism of the Roman Catholic Church and questioning of its beliefs. Its abuses were well-known. There were bishops who kept mistresses, abbots who lived lives of luxury, nuns who could not read and write and parish priests who neglected their duties. Instead of helping the poor, the Church made heavy financial demands which seemed to many to be little short of extortion.

In recent years, Martin Luther had been preaching the reformed doctrine in Germany, and Protestant beliefs were spreading. Copies of Protestants books and pamphlets came flooding into Scotland, both in merchants' ships arriving from the continent at east coast ports, and overland, in the packs of carriers travelling north from England. Indeed, Henry VIII had deliberately used Protestantism as well as bribery in his attempts to destabilise James V's Roman Catholic rule in Scotland. As a result, people were beginning to demand services in their own language instead of Latin, they wanted English translations of the Bible, and they claimed the right to have the wine as well as the bread at Communion, which would revert to being a simple service of commemoration. From time to time, Protestants travelled through East Lothian, spreading the reformed doctrine, and in the early days of 1546 a particularly charismatic preacher named George Wishart arrived in Haddington.

Chapter 2

THE SIEGE OF HADDINGTON

George Wishart was a native of Angus. Tall, thin and dark, he had the air of a fastidious scholar, but his powerful sermons had been drawing large crowds both in his home county of Angus and in the west of Scotland. Several attacks had recently been made on his life and, as a result, he now travelled with a bodyguard. In front of him walked a short, sturdy man carrying a big, two-handed sword for his protection. John Knox, a priest, had been born in Giffordgate, just across the river from St Mary's. He had studied at St Andrews University and after working as a notary in the Haddington area, he had become a Protestant. Now, he was Wishart's friend and fervent supporter.

Protestants sometimes managed to hold services in their parish church and, when Wishart came to Haddington, local people arranged that he should preach in St Mary's. On his first day, he delivered two sermons. In the morning there was a large congregation, but by afternoon the numbers had dwindled. Patrick, 3rd Earl of Bothwell, one of the local landowners, was a loyal Roman Catholic and when he had heard what was going on, he had ordered his tenants to stay away. Wishart spent that night at Lethington Tower (now Lennoxlove), the house of Sir Richard Maitland, before returning to St Mary's to preach again the following day before another sparse congregation. That afternoon, John Knox found him pacing up and down beneath the east window behind the high altar. Wishart was deeply troubled. He knew that the Roman Catholic authorities were closing in on him, his supporters in Lothian were deserting him and his followers in the west of Scotland had written to him cancelling a planned visit to Edinburgh. He wearied of the world, he told Knox sadly, for he believed that men were beginning to weary of God.

He preached his last sermon in the gathering gloom of that winter day, warning his hearers that a fearful fate awaited them if they ignored the word of God. He prophesied that if the townspeople did not mend their ways, Haddington would be plagued by fire and the sword, and occupied by foreigners. When he had finished, he said goodbye to his followers and then he went out of St Mary's. A hard frost had made it too dangerous to ride, and so he set off on foot to walk with a few friends to Ormiston, where he intended to spend the night. He did not, however, allow John Knox to go with him. 'One is sufficient for a sacrifice,' he told him ominously. A few hours later, Wishart was arrested. He was taken to St Andrews, tried for heresy and burned at the stake.

Cardinal Beaton had presided over Wishart's trial and execution and on 29 May 1546 he was murdered in his castle at St Andrews by a group of Protestants seeking revenge. The assassins

John Knox, a woodcut from Beza's *Icones*, believed to be the most authentic likeness of him. (*Scottish National Portrait Gallery*)

(right) Sir James Wilford, Governor of Haddington. Note the view of the town in the top right hand corner. *(Scottish National Portrait Gallery)*

occupied the castle and remained there until they were besieged and captured by a French fleet sent in response to Mary of Guise's pleas for assistance. The situation was becoming increasingly fraught and it seemed as if Scotland would become a battlefield for the English and the French. It was against this background that Somerset decided in the spring of 1548 to establish an English base in Haddington. From there, his soldiers could carry out raids on the surrounding countryside and they would be within striking distance of Edinburgh.

Lord Grey crossed the border on 21 February 1548 with several thousand men and two days later he was in Haddington. Writing to Somerset to announce his arrival, he reported that the nunnery had surrendered to him but he gave no account of how he had entered the town. It seems likely that he had encountered little if any resistance. Some of the inhabitants may have fled at his approach, some favoured England anyway, but for the most part the townspeople had long since learned that it was useless trying to hold out. By submitting they would save their lives and possibly their buildings. Grey decided against setting up his headquarters in St Mary's and installed himself in the tolbooth, which was well fortified with a moat and drawbridge. None of the people of Haddington has left us an account of what followed, but it is possible to piece together the progress of events from the various reports sent by the English military commanders and from descriptions by the French.

According to Grey, many Scots from the surrounding area came to him to offer their services. Henry VIII had always been lavish in his use of bribes and at least some of the lairds and gentlemen were genuinely convinced Protestants who welcomed Grey as their defender against their Roman Catholic fellow countrymen. He occupied himself by taking raiding parties to capture some of the important houses in the surrounding area: Yester, Saltoun and Herdmanston. He did not have enough men to garrison them and so he gave them into the keeping of those Scots whom he thought that he could trust, making sure that they gave pledges for their loyalty. He was, of course, well aware that the Scots would very soon try to recapture Haddington. His spies had reported that the Regent Arran and the Scottish army were marching south while the Earl of Argyll was mustering highland forces at Perth. Within days Arran and his men were in East Lothian, recapturing Saltoun and burning Ormiston.

George Wishart being burned at the stake in 1546, woodcut by an unknown artist. *(Glasgow University Library, Department of Special Collections)*

Lord Grey decided to ride to London to consult with Somerset in person about his next move. He set out in mid-March, by 6 April was back in Berwick, stayed on the Border for about three weeks and on 28 April was in Haddington once more. Somerset had told him to garrison the town, see to its defences and then return to Berwick, leaving a governor in command. Grey

ÆTATIS SVÆ 32
HADDINGTVN TOVN
AÑO DOMINNI 1547

(opposite) Plan of Haddington with Nungate from *Historic Haddington: the archaeological implications of development.* (*University of Glasgow, Department of Archaeology*)

accordingly recommended Sir James Wilford for the post, telling the Duke, 'There is no man among us so apt for that charge.' Another native of Kent, Wilford had also served with Grey in France and had fought bravely at Pinkie. Somerset authorised the appointment and Grey turned his attention to the defences of the town.

On 29 April he set out to survey the situation with yet another Kentish colleague who had served with him in France, Sir Thomas Palmer, an experienced engineer. There seems to have been no proper wall round the town and so they decided that they would have to build one. It should be of earth and turf, at least twenty feet high, with a parapet, in effect making Haddington into a large, square fort. It would have an earth and timber bastion faced with turf at each corner. These bastions came to be called after their commanders. In the north corner was Sir Robert Bowes's Bastion, in the east was the Abbey Bastion, Captain Wyndham's Bastion was at the south corner and at the west was Tiberio's Bastion, defended by Italian mercenaries. Cannon would be mounted on the top of the bastions.

Outside the wall, a round-bottomed dry ditch was to be dug, with a second ditch behind the outer rampart. Inside the town, more earthen walls would be constructed to block the gaps between the houses in Market Street, the High Street and Hardgate, and there would be a wall and a ditch running from north to south at the west end of the marketplace. The tolbooth would be strongly fortified with further earthen walls. If the Scots managed to break through the defences, the English garrison would retreat to this safe stronghold. Building of the walls, bastions and ditches began at once. Grey had told his men to clear from the area outside the defences all houses, walls and trees, anything that would give cover to the enemy.

St Mary's, of course, lay outside the new defences. Presumably when the English came, services had ceased and the priests and chaplains had retreated to their own houses. Somerset was a leading Protestant and everyone knew the damage his men had inflicted on Holyrood and on the Border abbeys. So what was to happen to St Mary's? Somerset himself had recognised its importance when he had suggested it as a possible headquarters for the English and Grey was very conscious of the fact that, if the enemy captured it, they could mount guns on the roof and fire directly into the town. On 21 May John Brende, who was in charge of the work, received a list of orders which included the instruction that the church of Haddington was to be taken down.

While his men dug ditches, constructed ramparts and began to dismantle St Mary's, Lord Grey captured Dalkeith Castle, set fire to Musselburgh and finally left for Berwick on 12 June. He went by way of Dunbar and while he stood watching it 'burn handsomely', as he put it, he sighted a fleet lying off the town and counted 120 sail. There were sixteen galleys, three great ships, a brigantine and many other small vessels. The French had answered Mary of Guise's pleas for further assistance. There were rumoured to be 10,000 men in the French force, led by the Sieur d'Essé. They landed at Leith and were soon marching to Musselburgh, dragging great cannon and field pieces with them.

On 20 June, St Mary's was said to be 'in manner down' and on 23 June Lord Grey was telling Somerset that the church was 'overthrown' and everything was ready for the enemy attack. By the end of June the fortifications were indeed finished, but St Mary's was still standing. The English had been interrupted in their efforts to demolish it by the arrival of the enemy. The Regent Arran had drawn up his army beside Lethington Tower and the French were camped three miles away, at Clerkington. Arran's men started to move down the slope towards Haddington, the English soldiers working at the church presumably withdrew into the town at their approach, and the Scots took possession of St Mary's.

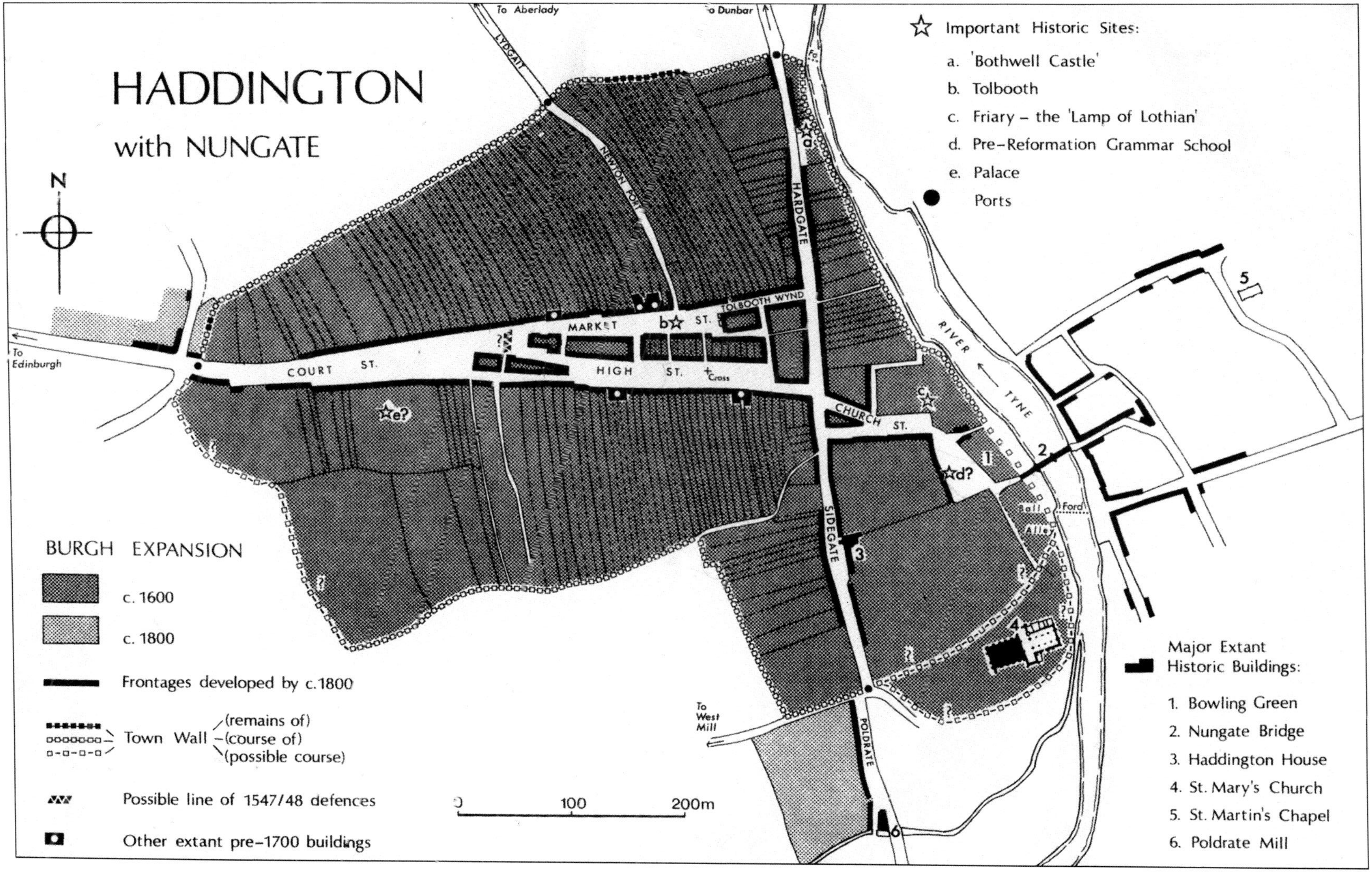

Based on the Ordnance Survey Map. (Courtesy of Historic Scotland).

Mary of Guise, attributed to Corneille de Lyon
(*Scottish National Portrait Gallery*)

On 2 July, Palmer and his colleague Sir Thomas Holcroft passed on to Somerset the latest report from Haddington, with interesting details about the state of the church. The walls were standing yet, and the enemy had begun firing into the town from the top of the steeple until the English guns fired back and stopped them. The vaults, meaning the roof arches, of both steeple and church were broken and the church was 'uncovered', in other words, roofless. Also, the pillars had been cut and underpropped, the Scots 'thinking they might have turned it over when they had list [when they wished]', but they had failed because 'the English ordnance beats through the steeple at every shot.' It has traditionally been said that the English did all the damage to St Mary's, but this letter from Palmer and Holcroft seems to imply that the Scots were responsible for undermining the church. Until some new evidence emerges, it is impossible to know exactly who did what, but there appears to be little doubt that the Scots continued the work that the English had begun. For both sides, St Mary's was no longer a house of God but a military vantage point in their struggle for the possession of Haddington.

By now the French were firing at Wyndham's bulwark and they brought more guns from Dunbar to attack the town from the mill at the back of the Franciscan Friary. The church is 'up still', Palmer and Holcroft noted regretfully on 3 July, with a great band of foot soldiers lying behind it and Scots, armed with the portable, long-barrelled guns called hackbuts or arquebuses, were at the top of the steeple again, shooting into the town with such effect that they damaged the tolbooth. The French continued to batter Wyndham's bastion and dug a deep trench to within 40 feet of the outer English ditch. Had they persisted, they would almost certainly have taken Haddington there and then, but politics intervened. Henri II of France was not assisting the Scots for philanthropic reasons. There was a price to be paid. Determined to bind Scotland to him as his ally once and for all, he had promised his help on condition that Mary, Queen of Scots should marry his eldest son, the Dauphin François. The Scots had agreed, but no formal treaty had been signed. Henri's commanders now let it be known that until that was done, they would not make their final assault.

Mary of Guise was alarmed and annoyed by this turn of events. Thirty-one years old, nearly six feet tall, with dark auburn hair, a fair complexion and grey-blue eyes, she had already suffered considerable tragedy in her life. She had been twice widowed, three of her sons had died in infancy and she had been forced to leave her only surviving boy behind in France when she married James V. Formidably intelligent and energetic, she had now dedicated herself to preserving Scotland for her little daughter, Mary, Queen of Scots and for her that meant maintaining both the French alliance and the Roman Catholic Church. Moreover, Mary of Guise wanted to rule Scotland as Regent herself, for she did not trust Arran. She had almost succeeded in wresting the regency from him in 1544, but although she was not yet powerful enough to displace him she was determined to do all she could to drive the English out of Scotland.

Gathering the members of the Scottish parliament, she rode at once to join Arran and d'Essé at the Cistercian nunnery where, on 7 July 1548, the Treaty of Haddington was duly signed. Mary, Queen of Scots would marry the Dauphin and in return Henri II would maintain and defend Scotland just as he did his own kingdom, while making sure that he preserved the ancient freedom and laws of the Scots. Mary of Guise then went to both the French and Scottish camps to address the soldiers and thank them for their efforts thus far. Anxious to know everything that was going on, she decided on the evening of 9 July to climb the tower of St Mary's for a better view of the siege.

According to contemporary accounts, guns from both sides were firing as she rode up to the back of the church and, at the very moment she arrived, there was a tremendous explosion. Seeing her cavalcade from a vantage point inside the town, the English gunners had taken aim with deadly accuracy. Sixteen members of the Queen's retinue fell dying around her, many more were injured and she herself fainted from shock. When she had recovered, she went back to Edinburgh to arrange the funerals of those who had been killed, and then at the end of the month she rode to Dumbarton, to part tearfully from her daughter and watch her embark for France.

In her absence, the siege of Haddington continued, the French and English mining and countermining while German mercenaries employed by the French were now in St Mary's, busily constructing a high timber platform at the top of the tower so that they could fire into the town even more effectively than before. The English failed to halt the work, despite Sir Thomas Palmer's claims that the Germans had been forced to stop because his guns had 'so beaten the stones about their ears'. A French and Scottish assault on the walls of Haddington was expected at any moment. Men, women and children from the surrounding area gathered to watch the action, but in the end the English managed to drive off the attackers.

Inside the town, supplies were running out. Wilford might boast that Haddington was six times stronger than it had been at the start, and needed only powder, shot and working tools, but before long the garrison were desperately short of food. At first the English sympathisers in the area had kept them well supplied, but that was no longer possible with the Scottish and French armies so close at hand. Some of the townspeople of Haddington were still prepared to co-operate, and later that year Wilford made a point of telling Somerset that two of the burgesses, George Forres and his cousin John Richenton, had suffered great losses but had served the English honestly throughout the siege.

The plight of the garrison was eased when an English fleet arrived in the estuary of the River Forth at the end of July and there was talk of the French withdrawing to defend Leith. Seizing his opportunity, Francis Talbot, 5th Earl of Shrewsbury, who was stationed on the Borders, rode north and managed to bring supplies and reinforcements into the town. In spite of this relief, Wilford remained short of money and his soldiers began to desert. The French had now taken up their winter quarters, but the Sieur d'Essé decided to try to surprise Haddington by night. He and his men managed to creep up as far as St Mary's Churchyard before the alarm was raised and they were driven off. Conditions in the town were now deteriorating rapidly, for plague had broken out and people were dying in the streets. The dwindling garrison were inadequately clad for the winter weather, they had no proper beds to sleep in and although they still went up to the walls to keep watch, they were exhausted.

Regardless of the problems being experienced by his men, Somerset urged further military action, writing to instruct Wilford to attack St Mary's. The Scots and French had apparently fortified it so strongly that taking it would require a major operation and Wilford felt that the season was too far advanced for him to attempt it. He did, however, promise to capture the church the following March, estimating that he would have to use more than three thousand soldiers to be sure of success. 'The place once taken,' he observed, 'is of great force.' Christmas came and went, the siege dragged on, but the planned seizure of the church did not take place. Wilford was wounded and taken prisoner during an expedition to attack Dunbar Castle. He was eventually exchanged for a Scottish prisoner, but he never fully recovered from his injuries and he did not return to Haddington. In November 1549 he was in York, 'very weak', and a year later he died.

French reinforcements arrived in Scotland not long after his capture, and in June 1549 began to construct a fort at Aberlady to prevent Haddington from being provisioned from there. They were confident now that they could starve out the English garrison and indeed there were reports that the soldiers were being forced to eat dogs and rats. Obviously the dreadful conditions were not confined to the garrison. The townspeople too must have been in a desperate state. Sir James Croft had replaced Wilford, and by 17 September 1549, he and the garrison were sending hourly pleas for help. The English authorities finally decided that they would have to evacuate this 'evil taken town' which had cost them so dearly in both men and money. Haddington had become 'an island in a sea of enemies', and it was not worth trying to hold it any longer.

Henry Manners, 2nd Earl of Rutland, Warden of the East and Middle Marches, marched north with an army of eleven thousand men and orders to remove the remaining garrison and munitions, destroy the fortifications and raze the town. Contrary to expectation, the Scots and the French made no move to intervene. There was, after all, little point in attacking the English when they were about to withdraw. Rutland and his men dismantled the fortifications completely, to prevent the Scots from making use of them, burned the Friary, set fire to the houses and finally marched away, carrying with them the three bells of St Mary's. After eighteen months, the longest siege in both Scottish and English history was over and the exhausted inhabitants were left to survey their ruined houses and their battered church.

Chapter 3

THE REFORMED CHURCH

It is difficult to determine the exact state of Haddington after the siege. The surviving burgh records are extensive and they begin early, with charters and writs recording gifts to St Mary's from the fifteenth century onwards, but between 1545 and 1551 all is silent. When the burgh court book resumes in March 1551, it is with the heartfelt award of an annual pension of 8 merks to Robert Maitland for life, 'for saving the evidents [records] of the burgh of Haddington'. The common good account amplifies this by noting that the payment to Robert was made 'for again getting of the whole evidents pertaining to the town out of the Englishmen's hands.' How he did it is not specified, but the sense of gratitude is palpable.

Subsequent pages of the court book give brief glimpses of the aftermath of destruction and the slow recovery. On 9 December 1554, for instance, John Forrest submitted his invoice for rebuilding the mills and cleaning the dams 'after the departure of the Englishmen out of the said burgh' and there are references to landholdings which had been burned. As late as 20 March 1579 Alexander Simpson, clerk of the sheriffdom of Edinburgh, was given a waste tenement at the east port, with the explanation that it had been burned 'by force and violence of the English'. As for St Mary's, the priests and chaplains presumably reclaimed their church as soon as the soldiers left, but they must have found the building in a sad state after its occupation by Scottish, French and German soldiers and its bombardment by English guns.

The reports sent to Somerset in the opening months of the siege had given the impression that the entire church was tottering on the verge of collapse, but that was wishful thinking and his later anxiety to capture it indicates that St Mary's had become something of a fortress. Nevertheless, the choir was in a bad way, with no roof and much damage to the stonework. Windows had been smashed, there was a great gap in the outer wall of the north aisle and the south wall of the church is pitted still with the marks of cannon balls and bullets. The nave seems to have been in a reasonable condition. No doubt emergency repairs were carried out, and services were resumed, but for many months everyone lived under the threat of a further English invasion.

James Hamilton, 2nd Earl of Arran, Duke of Châtelherault, attributed to A. Bronckorst.
(*The Hamilton Collection, Lennoxlove*)

This danger did not recede until 1553, when Edward VI of England died and was succeeded by his half-sister Mary I, a fervent Roman Catholic. The following year, Mary of Guise finally managed to wrest the regency of Scotland from the Earl of Arran, now Duke of Châtelherault, and the two Queens began a cautiously friendly correspondence. There were still outbreaks of trouble on the Borders, but otherwise prospects for Anglo-Scottish relations looked more promising than they had done for quite some time. Certainly the situation within

Lord James Stewart, later Earl of Moray in 1561, by Hans Eworth. (*In a Private Collection*)

Scotland remained highly volatile as more and more people converted to Protestantism, but Mary of Guise was making great efforts to restore peace and stability.

Encouraged by this improvement in the general atmosphere, the clergy of St Mary's redoubled their efforts to reclaim objects and revenues lost during the siege. On 25 June 1555 Martin Wilson was prosecuted in the burgh court for withholding a silver chalice belonging to the baker craft and the altar of St Aubert. Summoned to appear on 9 July, he failed to do so, nor did he hand over the chalice. Whether he was unscrupulously taking advantage of the recent chaos or whether he was merely engaged in one of the usual petty squabbles with the clergy is unclear. Again, on 7 July, John Crossar, chaplain of the altar of the Holy Blood, came to the court to sue Janet and Margaret Barns, heirs of the late John Barns, for money owed by Barns from his land on the north side of Tolbooth Street. Without their customary revenues, Crossar and the other chaplains would have had no means of subsistence.

For their part, the town council decided that the time had come to make a serious effort to repair their parish church. It would be extremely expensive to restore the choir but that was in any event the responsibility of the Priory of St Andrews. The Prior had been regrettably slow to act, but then he was not exactly a mature and experienced ecclesiastical administrator. Lord James Stewart, later Earl of Moray, was an illegitimate son of King James V. Like many other sons of important men, he had been given a living in the Church with a view to securing his financial future and he had been only seven years old when his father obtained his appointment as Prior of St Andrews. He was eighteen when the siege of Haddington ended. He was hardly likely to initiate any action, and those clerics who carried out his work for him had no desire to spend money on a church which lay in the path of any future invasion. As a result, nothing seems to have been done. In 1555, however, the town council decided to send Bernard Thomson as their representative to St Andrews to sue for the money they needed and soon afterwards he and two colleagues, James Oliphant and Adam Wilson, were dispatched to meet the Prior himself.

Lord James, by this time a handsome, intelligent twenty-four year old, was at court in attendance on his stepmother, Mary of Guise. Bernard and his colleagues therefore rode to Edinburgh where they spent five days. There is no record of the outcome of their meeting, and although later events suggest that the Prior gave them a sympathetic hearing, no building work on the choir seems to have followed. Forced to do something themselves, the council gave £20 that year to a Dutchman who 'brought timber to the kirk'. In June 1556 their treasurer paid for thirty-five oak joists delivered to Thomas Mauchlin for repair of the south aisle and in 1558 some work on the roof was authorised. In each case, it seems probable that the nave was receiving attention.

Late in 1558 a new crisis loomed when Mary I of England died and her Protestant half-sister, Elizabeth I, became queen. The Scottish Protestants rejoiced in the expectation that she would send them support, and indeed she did, if only after a good deal of initial procrastination. Hostilities broke out once more but fortunately for Haddington, the scene of military action lay elsewhere. Mary of Guise fortified Leith with French soldiers, and the English laid siege to the port. Seriously ill with chronic heart disease, the Queen Regent struggled on, but her Protestant subjects were becoming increasingly powerful and when in 1559 John Knox arrived back in Scotland from continental exile and preached a series of inflammatory sermons, there were public disturbances in Perth and elsewhere.

The Lords of the Congregation, as the Protestant leaders now called themselves, deprived Mary of Guise of the regency. Her few remaining supporters were deserting her by the day and the reinforcements promised to her by

legally entitled to their means of subsistence. They were forbidden to say Mass, but they were nevertheless permitted to gather in the money they had always received from parishioners for their maintenance and they were likewise allowed to stay where they were, living in the houses they had always occupied. There was no persecution of Roman Catholics.

In September 1560, Haddington town council ordered its treasurer to pay £6 a year to James Mauchlin, chaplain of the altar of St James, 'all the days of his life' and when he formally renounced his chaplaincy the following year, they gave him a special payment of £4 in addition to the £6 already assigned to him. When John Anderson, chaplain of the altar of the Three Kings of Cologne, found himself without accommodation he was told that he could build himself a small house on the north west part of the vicar's garden. Many priests lived out their lives in quiet retirement, but a surprising number became Protestant ministers. Indeed it has been estimated that well over fifty per cent of the staff of the Reformed Church were men who had been Roman Catholic clergy, former priests continuing to minister to the same congregation in the same church as before.

William Wilson of St Mary's had been clerk to both burgh and parish since 1535. On 26 March 1567 he presented a petition to the town council, pointing out that he had some time before agreed to a request that he should 'minister in the parish church with water at baptism', as well as keeping the kirk and its close clean and opening its doors at convenient times. Emphasising that he was 'a born bairn' of Haddington, William asked permission to collect twelve pence a year from 'each fine house' within the burgh. He had always done this in the past, he said, from the time of his first appointment in 1535 until the day when, as he somewhat tactlessly put it, 'the Imitation of Religion' was introduced' twenty-five years later. His terminology hardly suggests that he was a fervent Protestant. However,

the French failed to materialise. She finally died in Edinburgh Castle on 11 June 1560. The French had already decided that they had wasted enough men and money on Scotland and they would undoubtedly have come to terms with the English long before, had it not been for Mary of Guise's determination to fight on. The French and the English signed the Treaty of Edinburgh on 6 July 1560, agreeing that all foreign forces should withdraw and when the Reformation Parliament met that autumn, its members passed legislation making Scotland an officially Protestant country.

Even so, the structure of the old Church was not instantly swept away, nor were its bishops, priests and chaplains replaced by an entirely different Protestant personnel. There were far too few Protestant preachers available to act as ministers and while the Reformed Church would have liked to have had all Roman Catholic ecclesiastical revenues and property, that was simply not possible. Priests and chaplains were acknowledging dryly that he had indeed been officially employed before 'the Imitation of Religion' and noting that he was now willing to conform, the council decided to grant his request. They did so on condition that he fulfilled all his duties, sang the psalms each Sunday and acted as chanter (meaning precentor). They would also pay him eleven shillings a year for keeping the kirk clean.

The longstanding link between the Priory of St Andrews and St Mary's Church had obviously been broken by the Reformation, but Haddington town council continued to consult with Lord James Stewart. It was in their interests to maintain their connection with him, for he was now arguably the most important man in the kingdom. Shortly after his previous meeting in Edinburgh with Bernard Thomson and the others he had converted to Protestantism, becoming one of the leaders of the Lords of the Congregation and the friend of John Knox. On the return of Mary, Queen of Scots from France in August 1561, he acted as her principal adviser and the town council decided to approach him once more about money for the church repairs.

The east end of the building was deteriorating with every year that passed, and on 7 October 1561 the council was forced to rule that those who carried away stones from the church to repair their own houses would be fined eleven shillings. The following February, James Oliphant and Bernard Thomson had a meeting with Lord James in Edinburgh and on 2 March he signed a contract with them, promising them 600 merks for the repairs. This sum was not nearly enough to re-roof and repair the choir, but that was not the intention. According to tradition, John Knox had come up with the solution to the seeming insuperable problem. A barrier wall would be built, by using stones from the north transept to block up the arches at the east end of the nave. The choir and transepts could then be left in their ruined state, the barrier wall would hide what had become an eyesore and there was the added advantage that it would prevent the congregation from seeing where the high altar had stood. There were to be no reminders of the hated Mass.

It is uncertain precisely when the work was done. It is sometimes said that it was carried out in 1558 and an entry in the common good account for that year does record a payment to a mason 'to make holes in the pillars to let in the timber'. This could conceivably have referred to the construction of the barrier wall, but it was more probably connected with the roof repairs being done at the time. It should be remembered that if Knox really was responsible for the idea, he was out of the country in 1558. It is much more likely that he was involved in Lord James's discussions with the Haddington representatives in the early spring of 1562. Whenever the scheme was initiated, the barrier wall was duly erected and after that, services were held in the plain, rectangular space which had formerly been the nave.

There remained the question of finding a Protestant minister for St Mary's and it was no doubt Lord James who suggested one of his old teachers, Patrick Cockburn for the post. A native of Choicelee in Berwickshire, Patrick was now in his fifties. He had studied at the universities of St Andrews and Paris before entering the Roman Catholic Church and becoming a prebendary of Dunbar Collegiate Church. He apparently taught at St Andrews University and concurrently held the position of Professor of Oriental Languages, meaning Hebrew, at the Sorbonne. He seems to have numbered Lord James among his students at St Andrews. He was in his retinue when Lord James went to France in 1548 and he was there with him again ten years later, for the wedding of Mary, Queen of Scots to the Dauphin. One of the first books that he wrote was dedicated to Lord James, who rewarded him with a pension of £50 a year and in 1559, perhaps with his patron's encouragement, he converted to Protestantism.

The services Patrick conducted in St Mary's were, of course, very different from those of his Roman Catholic predecessors. Summoned by the bells of the tolbooth, since their own bells had been carried off, the congregation sat on benches facing each other across a central aisle. There were now no altars, statues or paintings, no richly embroidered vestments, sanctus bells or wafting incense. Latin chanting had gone and so too had the Latin Bible. Instead, services were in English, metrical psalms were sung without any accompanying organ and the parishioners listened to lengthy sermons. Because the reformers placed great emphasis on the preaching of the word of God, the focal point of the church was the pulpit.

On Communion day, plain wooden boards were brought in for the Lord's Supper, erected in the main aisle and covered with linen cloths. The congregation sat there to share the bread and wine in solemn remembrance of the Last Supper. There was no longer any miraculous transformation of the bread and the wine into the body and blood of Christ, although these elements continued to be regarded as nourishment for the soul. In Calvin's Geneva, ministers celebrated Communion every week, but Scottish Protestants followed the example of the Swiss reformer Zwingli and the Lord's Supper was held four times a year in towns and three times a year in the country. The dates were carefully chosen to avoid Easter and the other festival days of the Catholic Church.

Patrick Cockburn stayed at St Mary's until his death in 1568. There seems to have been some difficulty in finding a replacement for him, as the Church was still in a transitional phase. Mary, Queen of Scots did not ratify the Reformation Parliament's legislation until 1567, proper financial provision for the ministers would not come until the Regent Morton's period of government in the 1570s and there were still not enough properly qualified ministers. During the vacancy at St Mary's, Andrew Simpson took services. He was exhorter at Bolton, which meant that he could preach although he could not administer the sacraments. Anxious to have a proper replacement for Patrick Cockburn, in the spring of 1570 Haddington town council decided to send Provost John Ayton to Edinburgh with either the invaluable Bernard Thomson or James Cockburn 'to get an answer about the minister'.

Their efforts were successful, and on 25 August they sent John Douglas to bring their new minister to the town in time for the next Sunday service. James Carmichael had previously been schoolmaster of St Andrews Grammar School and for a time he acted as both schoolmaster in Haddington and minister of St Mary's. The work was really too much for one man, and in 1571 the town council gave orders that all annuities belonging to the chaplains and altars in the burgh were to be collected and used as a salary for a schoolmaster. None seems to have been appointed, however, and James continued to combine both roles until 1576. He stayed on as minister until 1628, apart from an interval of ten years from 1587-97 when his support of opponents of James VI led him to seek shelter in England.

Soon after James Carmichael's appointment, repairs and improvements were set in hand. Ever since the siege, the windows had been in a bad state, and now Andrew Lyall was sent to Leith to find a good glazier, probably William Aytoun, who was later made a burgess of Haddington in recognition of the fact that he had put glass in the church windows. In the interests of economy, it was decided to make use of fifty feet of the old glass, some of it from the choir windows, and John Campbell was employed to take it down and move it to the nave. New glass was purchased at the cost of two shillings a foot, and John Stevenson cut it to size on three wooden planks provided for the purpose. He then put up the scaffolding and set the new glass in place after Henry Campbell had replaced the old beams in the windows.

While the glazier was at work, repairs to the wall round the churchyard were also effected. Parts of the dyke had fallen down and people were in the habit of pasturing their animals in the

One of the seventeenth century silver communion cups. (*Glasgow Museums and Art Galleries*)

churchyard. A new dyke was erected, with styles which would allow the parishioners access but keep out their livestock. George Hastie and Robert Dodds hewed stones for the dyke and John Gray carted them to the churchyard and brought a sack of sand on a horse's back. Henry Campbell built the dyke, and when he had done, he moved inside the church to put up a pillar of repentance. Before the Reformation, wrongdoers had to kneel before the high altar wearing linen clothes and carrying a candle, which they would present when they confessed their guilt. Now, there was a strict system of discipline enforced by the Kirk Session, the laymen chosen to be elders. Wrongdoers who were convicted of adultery, for example, would have to stand in sackcloth at the pillar of repentance during the service, so that everyone could see them.

In November 1572 the nave received a new floor when the burned Franciscan Friary in the town was finally demolished and paving stones were brought from it and laid in St Mary's. Work then went ahead on the nave roof. Local tenants were instructed to cart large quantities of slates to the church, two new joists were brought from Aberlady, sand and lime were supplied, stones for the vaulting of the roof were carried in and a lintel stone for the north door was put in place. Finally, on 14 June 1574, the masons and wrights were given drinksilver to celebrate 'the upsetting of the kirk', presumably meaning the re-roofing. Major repairs to the tower would follow in 1605.

With the church now wind and watertight, improvements could be made to the interior and in June 1575 the town treasurer was ordered to buy timber for new seats and a new pulpit. The following April 1576, Henry Campbell's pillar of repentance was for some reason replaced with one made of wood. Even that proved unsatisfactory, and on 5 April 1609 the town council decided that because the pillar of repentance was 'ower little', and the number of adulterers and fornicators was increasing 'daily', an additional pillar would have to be put up at the west end of the kirk, specifically for the adulterers. On a happier note, the church some years later acquired two pairs of fine new silver Communion cups, specially made by Patrick Borthwick in Edinburgh and engraved with the words, 'For the Kirke of Haddintoune 1645'.

Chapter 4

LOFTS AND VAULTS

By this time, Scotland was torn apart by civil war. Charles I's ecclesiastical policies had aroused great opposition and his desire for an episcopal form of church government, with powerful bishops and a prayer book based on the English model, was bitterly opposed by those who preferred a presbyterian system of church courts and supported the National Covenant. The arguments over bishops raged long after the King had been executed and his son Charles II restored to the throne. At St Mary's, James Forman, minister from 1677-1702, was an Episcopalian, but his successors were Presbyterian.

During the eighteenth century, the ecclesiastical arguments took a different turn, Burghers and Anti-Burghers and then Old Lights and New Lights arguing over the relationship between church and state. The vexed question of whether the local landowners, or heritors as they were known, should have a say in the selection of ministers finally culminated in the Disruption of 1843, when Thomas Chalmers led more than a third of the ministers out of the Church of Scotland to found the Free Church.

Throughout these turmoils, the choir and transepts of St Mary's stood open to the skies, a visible reminder of past conflict, a sad if romantic ruin haunted by owls, starlings and other birds which, the parishioners complained in 1625, were molesting 'the kirk and the people resorting thereto.' The shattered east end did serve one useful purpose, however. Before the Reformation, people of importance had been buried in the choir, the most illustrious immediately in front of the high altar. The reformers were anxious to put an end to this practice, which seemed to them to smack of popery. Indeed, the First Book of Discipline, compiled by John Knox and his colleagues, stated that no one was to have a burial service at all. Few people were happy with this, and so thanksgiving services for the lives of faithful Protestants were permitted. Indeed, Knox himself preached the sermon at the funeral of his friend the Regent Moray, assassinated in 1571, and Moray was interred inside the Church of St Giles in Edinburgh. Perhaps encouraged by this example, Thomas Punton petitioned Haddington Town Council three years later and was allowed to have a sepulchre in St Mary's, 'with his mark on it', because of his past good services.

In 1581, however, the General Assembly of the Church of Scotland forbade burial within churches altogether. People apparently paid little heed, for the order had to be repeated no fewer than four times between 1585 and 1643. It never did become law, despite the fact that King James VI personally supported a 1593 proposal that every nobleman should build a sepulchre for himself and his family outside their church. At St Mary's, the position was simpler, for well-to-do parishioners could satisfy themselves and at the same time avoid the censure of the General Assembly by constructing tombs in the ruined choir and transepts. The Brouns of Colstoun and the Sinclairs of Stevenson, for example, continued to bury their dead in the choir. Both families had long been associated with St Mary's. As early as 1457 the Brouns of Colstoun had given a legally binding assurance that they would make financial contributions towards the repair of the church, the construction of the choir and the furnishing of the high altar, while the Sinclairs had been patrons of the altar of the Holy Blood.

King James VI's friend and Lord Chancellor, John, 1st Lord Maitland, lived at Lethington (Lennoxlove) and was allowed to use the old sacristy at St Mary's as his mortuary aisle. To the north of the choir, it had been the place where the church plate and vestments were kept before the Reformation and it was there that the priests had robed themselves for services. When Lord Maitland died in 1595 he was buried in the vault beneath, his wife Lady Isabella Seton lay there too, and as time passed his son, John, 2nd Lord Maitland and his wife, Lady Jane Fleming, joined them. The aisle was re-roofed in about 1600 at the Maitlands' expense and a splendid monument in black marble and alabaster was put up in about

1675, with the recumbent figures of the two lords and their ladies slumbering peacefully in almost medieval state. Their virtues and achievements are described on black panels behind them and their colourful, gilded coats of arms with the lion rampant of Scotland adorn the open pediment above.

This monument was presumably commissioned by John Maitland, 1st Duke of Lauderdale. Born at Lethington Tower in 1616, he rose to rule Scotland with almost vice-regal powers on behalf of King Charles II. A big, arrogant man, nicknamed 'Red John' from the colour or his hair, he made himself highly unpopular in Scotland. After his second marriage, he decided that Lethington was no longer grand enough for him, and built for himself the new castle of Thirlestane, at Lauder. In the end, his corrupt government collapsed and he died, disgraced, in Tunbridge Wells in 1682. His body was brought home for burial in the family vault in St Mary's, more than two thousand horsemen attending the funeral in April 1683. Neither his widow nor his daughter by his first wife made any effort to erect a monument for him.

Presbyterians frowned on the idea of tombs with effigies of the deceased, preferring tablets with dignified inscriptions and in 1682 when William Seton, Provost of Haddington, was buried in the north transept of St Mary's, his handsome monument bore no image of himself but an elegant Latin inscription. During his ten years of office he had actually been imprisoned in Edinburgh Tolbooth on the orders of the Scottish Privy Council after he had bullied, arrested and illegally held George Seton of Barns and John Hay of Aberlady in Haddington Tolbooth, but his epitaph praised him for his 'fidelity, prudence and moderation', declaring him, perhaps a trifle defensively to have been 'altogether averse to covetousness, revenge, injustice or hatred against his fellow citizens'.

There was, of course, a limit to the number of people who could be buried at the east end of the church and those local landowners who were not permitted to use the choir or transepts had vaults as close to the building as they could manage. Probably using stones from the ruined east end, they constructed walls to enclose their plots, and the north wall of the church in particular was soon all but concealed by these enclosures. In 1659 more stones were carried away from the ruin to repair the fifteenth-century Nungate Bridge and, as the years went by, part of the choir was used to store spades, wheelbarrows and other tools, surplus earth was piled up there and wooden lean-to buildings were propped up against the walls.

Inside the nave itself, lack of space was already becoming a problem. St Mary's was, after all, almost half its former size and there was simply not enough room for all the worshippers. With no opportunity of expanding outwards, the only possibility was to build galleries where extra seating could be put in. These galleries did not run the length of the church. They were relatively small, for specific families or groups of people, and they were known as lofts. It had become customary for local landowners to sit in their own lairds' lofts, and in May 1603 the Haddington magistrates decided that they too would like to have a loft. They already had their own pew, but an elevated position would not only give them a better view but it would make them more visible to the ordinary townspeople. They had seen this sort of arrangement elsewhere, and when they commissioned the work to be done they specified that their loft was to be as finely wrought as any in the college kirk of Edinburgh or the kirk of Leith.

Constructed by three local wrights, Daniel, James and Laurence Cockburn, the magistrates' loft was built at the east end of St Mary's, presumably against the barrier wall. There were to be three seats, one behind the other, each three feet broad and one and a half feet higher than the seat in front of it, to ensure an unrestricted view. The front of the loft was to be of fine wainscot panelled with clapboard, each panel edged with an ornamental moulding. Access would be by means of a small stair. Sir William Seton of Kylesmuir, a local landowner and burgess of the town, was

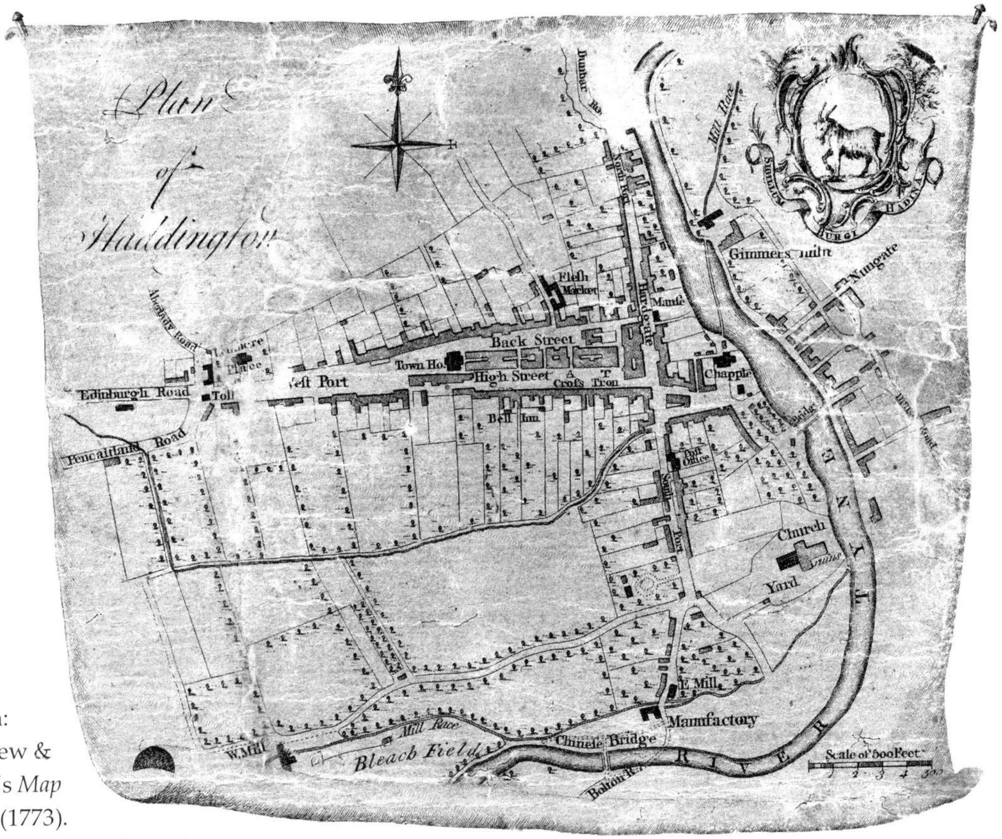

Plan of Haddington: vignette from Andrew & Mostyn Armstrong's *Map of the Three Lothians* (1773). (*East Lothian Council's Museum Service*)

evidently impressed, for he persuaded the magistrates to allow him and his family to sit at the north end of the loft, separated from them by a partition which he would put up at his own expense.

The Trades Incorporations were quick to see their opportunity. Deprived of their pre-Reformation privilege of endowing their own altars, they decided that they could make their presence felt in St Mary's by having their own lofts. They required the permission of the town council, of course, but the council were willing enough to agree, provided each incorporation paid for the work to be done. The wrights and masons were the first to apply, and they built their loft at the east end of the north side of the church. Far from solving the problem, however, the construction of further lofts led to endless trouble. In November 1614, the bakers were told to take down their new loft on the south side of the church because they had not been given permission to put it there, and it was keeping out the light. Feelings ran high, and on 10 December John Vallance, a mason and town councillor, was assaulted by two of the baker incorporation under cover of darkness because they blamed him for having taken down their original seat in the church.

By 1615, Sir William Seton had become unhappy with his location. Because 'the pulpit and the most part of the whole seats of the said kirk being changed', he was no longer in a prime position and he persuaded the wrights and masons to exchange lofts with him. That same year Mr George Grier, minister of St Martin's Church in the town, was involved in an unpleasant incident. He took some of the services at St Mary's and he was threatened by the hammermen when their loft was dismantled. They seem to have blamed him, although in fact the town council had ordered its removal. William Stoddart, one of their number, shouted abuse at Mr Grier and his wife from his window and was in consequence made to sit in the stocks at the Cross and then publicly repent in church before being imprisoned for his offence. Two years later, when the bakers and hammermen submitted a petition asking permission to build a new loft at the west end of the kirk, Mr Grier hastily supported their request.

VIEW OF THE PRIORY CHURCH AT HADDINGTON.

A Scene in an Old Gothic Church 22d Octr 1809

(above left) Engraving of St Mary's c1787. *(East Lothian Council Library Service)*
(below left) A Scene in an Old Gothic Church, satirising the incident involving George Harley. (*East Lothian Council Library Service*)

Not only were lofts clustering around the east and west ends of the church. By 1670 the masons and wrights were dissatisfied with their new position and they built an entirely new loft above their previous one. Others followed suit, until by the end of the eighteenth century the lofts were in places three tiers deep. Each of the Trades Incorporations by then had in front of its loft a painting indicating to whom the loft belonged. The colourful religious imagery of the Middle Ages had long since gone, but the austere Presbyterian interior of St Mary's was now enlivened by symbols of local activity, linked with suitably moral texts. The bakers sat proudly behind a picture of a wheat sheaf, with beams and scales for weighing dough, and the words, 'Bread is the staff of life'. The smiths displayed a representation of an anvil, hammer and horseshoes, while the fleshers had a fierce looking bull's head and the weavers' insignia was a loom, with the words, 'Improve your time, it is but little, 'tis swifter than a weaver's shuttle'

Haddington suffered an economic decline in the seventeenth and the early eighteenth centuries, but the coming of the stagecoach improved the town's prosperity and in the mid 1790s the number of parishioners attending the June Communion rose to over 990. Patrick Borthwick's silver cups were no longer adequate for such a large congregation, and the records note that in 1791 the Kirk Session were using two brass plates for the bread and five flagons for the wine. Various modest improvements were also made to the building. In 1797, after complaints about the ruinous state of the pulpit it was rebuilt, new furnishings were provided for it in 1800 and the interior of the church was whitewashed. Meanwhile, quarrels over the seating arrangements continued unabated.

Perhaps the most colourful wrangle over who should sit where occurred in October 1805. As a courtesy, the convener of the deacons of trades had for some years past been allowed to sit with the magistrates in their special pew. That autumn the deacons elected a new convener, George Harley, a local copper and tinsmith. For some unknown reason, the magistrates loathed George and when Sunday came they ordered the town's officer to bar the entrance to the pew when they saw him coming. Naturally enough, George was disconcerted but, not to be defeated, he simply marched down into the body of the church and then clambered over the pews in front until he reached his desired place. The magistrates were furious and, ignoring the fact that the minister was about to start the service, they protested loudly. A fracas broke out, and it was some time before order was restored.

The incident caused a good deal of horrified amusement throughout the town and gave rise to a humorous print entitled 'A Scene in an Old Gothic Church', but questions of status apart, the lack of space had once more reached a crisis point. Between 1801 and 1807 more than a thousand people were attending the June Communion. It was even suggested that the entire church should be demolished and a new building put up instead. This was out of the question. It would have been prohibitively expensive. Instead, it was decided to heighten the nave so that still more lofts could be inserted. Archibald Elliot, the architect of St Paul's Episcopal Church (now St Paul's and St George's) in York Place, Edinburgh was retained and work began in 1810. All the existing lofts were dismantled, amidst lively protests from their customary occupants. The local masons employed in the church included William Warburton from Haddington, Alexander Rutherford from Ormiston and Thomas Fraser from House-of-Muir, near Ormiston and while they were undertaking the work, they found embedded in the old masonry two masons' chisels and a wright's, presumably the tools of their medieval predecessors.

The capitals or upper parts of the great columns in the nave were taken down and six feet four inches of stonework added to the height of the pillars. The capitals were then replaced. The lateral walls of the church had to be correspondingly heightened too, gaining a further three feet with an open embattled parapet on top. The buttresses also became taller, some of the window tracery was renewed and the masonry under the arches on the east wall of the nave was rebuilt. The masons had to remove the original rib-vaulted roofs of the side aisles, replacing them with plaster ceilings. The interior was then given two coats of plaster to guard against damp, the great columns and their capitals were painted and the arches were given a coat of size. New panelled doors were put up at the west end.

The new pulpit, a high wooden structure with a canopy, was placed in the same position as its predecessor, between two pillars on the south side of the church. Immediately in front of it was the desk for the precentor, who led the congregation in the singing of the psalms. Because there was no artificial lighting in the church, two large candlesticks were placed on either side of the pulpit desk. New, squarish box pews had been installed, each with a table, and when Communion took place, portable divisions between them were removed and the individual tables were joined up to form one long table with seats on both sides. Stairs near the church entrance led to new galleries running round the north, east, west and parts of the south side, the magistrates occupying the front of the north gallery, so that they were opposite the pulpit.

While all this refurbishment was taking place, services were held in the nearby Anti-Burgher Secession Church, which was rented for this purpose at a cost of £50 a year. The entire project was completed by 1 March 1812, when the Reverend Dr Robert Lorimer and the Reverend Dr William Sibbald conducted a special service. A small commemorative baptismal bowl is inscribed with the words, 'The Church of Haddington, having undergone a thorough repair, was opened on Saturday the 1st March 1812, when the Reverend Robert Lorimer LLD, the senior clergyman, delivered a very suitable discourse from Exodus 20 verse 24, "In all places where I record my name I will come to thee and I will bless thee."' Dr Sibbald chose as his text, 'How dreadful is this place, this is none other but the House of God and this is the gate of Heaven.' The inscription goes on, 'It is nearly two years since the repairs were begun and are finished in a style of elegance which reflects the greatest honour on the heritors at whose expense they have been done, on the architect who planned them and on the tradesman who have executed them. The repairs cost five thousand pounds sterling.'

Overshadowing all the internal improvements, however, was the state of the disused east end. Gilbert Burns, brother of Robert Burns the poet, was factor at Lennoxlove and when he became an elder of St Mary's in 1808 he was particularly concerned about the ruin. There were fears that the tower might collapse on to the nave, with catastrophic consequences. To try to prevent a disaster, supporting wooden beams were stretched across the choir in the late eighteenth or early nineteenth century, in an effort to stop the walls from caving in. Not until 1858, however, were some repairs undertaken by the Commissioners of Works, and in 1864 the unsightly old wooden beams were replaced with iron rods. In spite of these precautions, an examination in 1884 would show that the church tower was eleven and a half inches off the plumb, the east gable nine inches off

In 1865-6 the tools and lean-to shacks were finally cleared away from the choir interior, it was sown with grass, an iron railing was put up around it, and unsightly stone walls enclosing landowners' graves on the north side of the church were demolished. The north side of the Lauderdale aisle was partly rebuilt, and new mullions and tracery were installed in the windows on that side. The year 1866 also saw the funeral of Jane Welsh, the wife of the celebrated historian, Thomas Carlyle. Highly intelligent, Jane was herself an accomplished writer as her

Plan of St Mary's.
(McGibbon & Ross: *The Ecclesiastical Architecture of Scotland.* 1896)

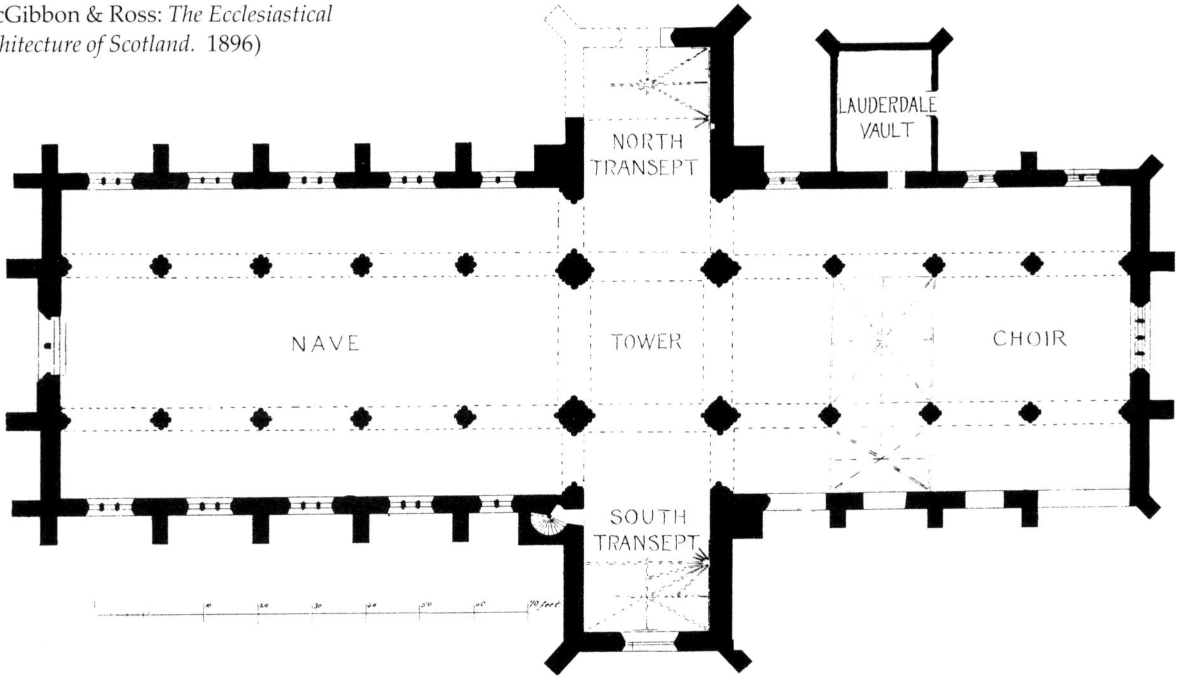

voluminous correspondence plainly shows. She and Thomas were both difficult people but they were devoted to each other, and when she died suddenly in London he composed a touching epitaph for her. Her father, a local doctor, was buried in St Mary's and her grave in the choir became a place of pilgrimage for her many literary admirers.

Meanwhile the heritors and congregation continued to wrestle with the problem of repairs. In 1877, new mullions and tracery were put in the great east window as a memorial to the Reverend Dr John Cook, who had been minister from 1833-74. The stone for the windows was brought from Garvald, and the work was done by a local builder, Peter Ormiston. Fifteen years later, the south window in the south transept was restored by the Earl of Wemyss in memory of his father and the west window was repaired by Dr Thomas Howden in memory of his wife Agnes and their son Thomas, also a doctor of medicine. This time, the stone came from Dumfriesshire, probably from Locharbriggs.

Some years after he came to St Mary's, the Reverend Dr Robert Nimmo Smith initiated a major new programme of alterations to the nave. A graduate of Edinburgh University, Dr Nimmo Smith had been ordained as minister of Cargill in 1870, coming to the second charge at St Mary's in 1875. In 1880 he took over the first charge and the following year his wife died, leaving him with two small children, Robert and Mabel. He remarried in 1883 and with his second wife, Mary Anne Tod, he had three daughters, Frances, (Mary) Dorothea and Hilda, and a son, Austin.

Devoted to St Mary's, Dr Nimmo Smith would have liked to see the entire church restored, and in 1891 he embarked upon a bold scheme of alterations intended to solve the accommodation problems once and for all. Yet again, the interior of the church would be heightened, this time by lowering the floor. The interior was emptied, the stone flags were removed and soil was dug out to reveal the base of the pillars. While this was being done, large quantities of human bones were found, probably from the burial ground of the original twelfth-century church. A new floor of red pine blocks was laid on a foundation of cement and asphalt. A modest entrance vestibule was formed at the west end by screening off a small part of the nave, and oak benches covered with red felt patterned with fleur-de-lis were installed. Two intricately carved galleries were now erected, one at the east end, one at the west. The east gallery, against the barrier wall, was for the organ and choir, with the communion table in front of it. The west gallery provided additional seating, with the magistrates occupying the front row.

Just as they had always done from the time of the Middle Ages, members of the congregation gifted furnishings for the interior. Two sisters, Jane and Helen Aitchison of Alderston, presented a handsome new communion table, pulpit, font and lectern. Sandstone from Dumfriesshire, probably of the fine variety known as Moat sandstone, was used in their construction. The marble communion table with its carved vines was placed on a platform of matching polished Italian rose-coloured marble veined with pale olive-green surrounded with white marble. The rise of the steps to the table was grey-blue and the treads were white.

The elaborate pulpit with its carved vines and biblical quotations rests on six marble shafts on top of a circular disk. It was placed beside one of the pillars on the north side of the nave. The marble lectern is surmounted by a brass eagle with outspread wings and the font has marble pillars with carved capitals and arches. All the carving on the communion table, pulpit, baptismal font and lectern and on the corbels under the galleries was undertaken by the brothers John and W. Birnie Rhind, both famous sculptors. Among their assistants was James Knox from Garvald, who worked on the pulpit and James Donaldson of Haddington made the minister's chair at the communion table.

St Mary's was re-opened on 16 June 1891 with a service conducted by Dr Nimmo Smith and the Reverend William Proudfoot, the Reverend Dr James MacGregor of St Cuthbert's Church, Edinburgh preaching the sermon. George Amos sang a solo which had been composed by Margaret, the sister of Jane and Helen Aitchison. The following year, a new organ was installed by Foster and Andrews of Hull, and inaugurated on 16 December 1892 with a recital by the newly appointed organist, W. Stewart. That same year, a programme of installing new stained glass windows began. Once again, these were the gifts of members of the congregation, in memory of relatives. Jane and Helen Aitchison provided the first window, by Alexander Ballantine of Edinburgh, showing the appearance of the Herald Angel to the shepherds. Jane died not long afterwards and in 1893 Helen presented another window by Ballantine, depicting the vision of St John the Divine, in memory of her sisters. The series continued until 1945, when it was completed with a window by William Wilson, celebrating divine wisdom, heavenly beauty and truth, and depicting King David writing his Psalms. It was given by Mrs H.D. Drysdale in memory of her parents, John Stirling a well-known local solicitor and his wife, Marion Murray.

Beautiful though the new windows of St Mary's were, there remained considerable anxiety about the state of the tower and the transepts. There were no funds for major repair work, but in 1902, John Christie of Cowden, a local benefactor, offered to donate the substantial sum of £7,500 towards the restoration of both tower and transepts. Dr Nimmo Smith was delighted. Architectural plans were drawn up and the Board of Works considered the feasibility of the proposals but all that took time and, before anything could actually be done, John Christie died. He left generous sums of money to found children's homes at Carmondean, Tenterfield and Templedean, but his will did not mention any bequest to St Mary's. Dr Nimmo Smith was deeply disappointed. In 1906, despairing of ever being able to do anything with the east end, the church authorities executed a deed of guardianship transferring responsibility for the ruins to the Ministry of Works. Six years after that, Dr Nimmo Smith died, his final ambition for St Mary's unachieved.

Chapter 5

A VISION FOR THE FUTURE

In 1922 a stone fell from the masonry and chipped off a small corner of the flat tombstone of Dr John Welsh, Jane Welsh Carlyle's father. Obviously it was not going to be safe for tourists to visit Jane's own grave nearby until something was done. Architects from the Ministry of Works examined the building and discovered that, although the tower was still at the same angle, the east gable was now eleven inches off the plumb. They carried out further tests during the following four years, and came to the conclusion that St Mary's was sinking. An underground flow of water was carrying away silt to the river and thereby undermining the entire building. New foundations would be needed if a catastrophe were to be averted, and work began in 1926.

To secure the stonework of the exterior walls and gables, all the wallheads had to be stabilised. The pillars at the west side of the crossing were in a reasonable condition, for at that side the tower was being supported by the sturdy barrier wall. Several of the other pillars, however, particularly those at the east end of the aisles, were off plumb by up to twelve inches and the Ministry of Works decided that, to prevent any further movement from the vertical, great blocks of concrete would have to be inserted underneath them. First of all, temporary brick piers were put in to support the arches and the walls while the work was being done, and then the foot of each pillar was cut through so that a cross section could be removed for examination. A number of the pillars were found to have a tree trunk at their core. This timber was carefully removed and the cavities where the wood had been were filled with concrete. After that, the concrete rafts were put in place and the strengthened pillars were positioned on top of these new foundation blocks. The temporary brick piers were then taken away. When the work on the foundations was complete, a collar of concrete was constructed round the wallheads of the entire east end.

All this took four years, and even when it was done, the Ministry of Works architects were well aware that the River Tyne remained a problem. It had been flooding Haddington for centuries, and there was no way of preventing that from continuing. It was imperative to keep a watch on the situation and take action as soon as there was any further sign of subsidence. The architect in charge therefore placed in the arches and gables of the east end pieces of mortar called 'tell-tales'. If these cracked or moved, it would mean that the building was sinking again. The repairs were tested in 1948 when there was another serious flood. A hundred and fifty families from the Nungate and other low-lying areas in the town had to be re-housed when the river burst its banks. The Lauderdale Vault was flooded to a depth of three or four feet, and when John McVie, the town clerk, went to inspect the damage, he was met by a macabre scene, for several of the coffins were floating in the water. The strengthened pillars of St Mary's, however, stood firm on their new concrete foundations

The River Tyne subsided, the vault dried out and the daily life of the church continued undisturbed. Parishioners attended services as their predecessors had been doing for the past eight hundred years. There were baptisms, marriages and funerals, and tourists and visitors came and went, walking round the handsome Victorian interior, poring over Thomas Carlyle's inscription on his wife's grave and gazing with mingled admiration and regret at the ruins, which were now an official Ancient Monument. 'Destroyed in the siege of Haddington in 1548', they read in their guide books, but although some may have felt a twinge of indignation, for most people these past conflicts seemed very long ago. Few could envisage the choir as it had once been, and fewer still imagined that the church would ever be restored to its former medieval proportions. One day in 1963, however, something happened which initiated a chain of events leading to the most exciting phase in the history of St Mary's.

The minister, the Reverend James Thomson, received a letter from Hilda, the youngest

Interior view of St Michael's Church, Linlithgow, photocopy of picture which inspired John McVie with the desire to see St Mary's restored. (*Scotsman Publications*)

THE SCOTSMAN, MONDAY, MA

NEW FURNISHINGS DEDICATED

Looking down the aisle to the chancel at St Michael's Church, Linlithgo where new carpeting and lighting were dedicated yesterday at t morning service by the minister, the Rev. David Steel. They were gift as a memorial to Mr John Smith, formerly of Woodside House, Linlithgo by his daughter, Mrs Hodgeton. The carpet incorporates the insign of St Michael, the shield, the dragon and the spear, and is 70 feet lon

daughter of Dr Nimmo Smith. After her father's death more than fifty years earlier, she and her sister had moved to Edinburgh. Now seventy-two years old, Hilda had inherited money from a relative who had made a fortune building railways in Canada and she felt that she would like to have her father commemorated in some way in the church where he had been minister for thirty-seven years. After careful thought, she decided that the best way of doing this would be to have a bell hung in the church tower in his memory. She would, of course, bear all the costs, but she was adamant that her name should be kept secret. The bell would be an anonymous donation. The minister was happy to agree to the plan, for he knew how much Dr Nimmo Smith had done for St Mary's, but because the tower was in the care of the Ministry of Works, he had to put the proposal to them. They replied at once that it would not be structurally safe to hang a bell in the tower. Disappointed, Hilda asked the minister to find some other way of commemorating her father and after some consideration he suggested a new church hall. The existing building, in Newton Port, was inconveniently far from St Mary's. Hilda was happy with this idea, and offered to donate £20,000 towards the erection of a new hall.

The Kirk Session set up a subcommittee to find a suitable site. John McVie was its convener. An energetic man of vision and enthusiasm, he was a solicitor with an old established law firm in Haddington as well as being town clerk and an elder of St Mary's, and he immediately identified a suitable piece of ground. Next to the churchyard stood seventeenth-century Haddington House, formerly owned by Harry Faunt and his brother, who sold the produce from the orchard and garden in their fruiterer's shop in Haddington. About twelve years before, John McVie's firm had acted for the Earl of Wemyss and March when both house and grounds were acquired for East Lothian Antiquarian and Field Naturalists' Society. John spoke to Lord Wemyss, who enlisted the support of Lady Broun Lindsay of Colstoun, President and Chairman of the Antiquarian Society and a site in the south east corner of the orchard was selected. At Hilda Nimmo Smith's suggestion, Alan Reiach, an Edinburgh architect, was commissioned to design the building. He estimated that it would cost about £40,000.

It seemed that everything was settled. St Mary's would have a handsome new church hall, Dr Nimmo Smith would be commemorated not only by the hall itself but by a memorial archway leading from it into the adjoining Lady Kitty's Garden and Hilda was persuaded to abandon her carefully guarded anonymity. A few days later, however, on 30 March 1964, John McVie opened his newspaper, *The Scotsman*, over breakfast and found himself looking at a striking photograph of the interior of St Michael's Church in Linlithgow. Taken from the west door, the picture showed the entire length of the nave to the far end of the choir. John had only once visited St Michael's, to attend the funeral of one of his old schoolmasters just after the Second World War, but he had been much impressed.

Now, as he gazed at the newspaper image, he found himself noticing the strong resemblance to St Mary's. From his pew at its west end, he looked each Sunday at a very similar view, but a much foreshortened one. Instead of being able to see right to the east end of his own church, he could see only as far as the barrier wall with its organ gallery, screening the ruins which lay beyond. In that moment, he suddenly thought how wonderful it would be if, rather than using Hilda's money to build a new hall, they could put it towards a complete restoration of St Mary's, removing the barrier wall, re-roofing the ruins and recreating the magnificence of Scotland's largest medieval church. The rebuilt choir and transepts would provide the additional space needed for congregational activities.

When he passed the paper across the table to his wife Lindsaye, saying to her excitedly, 'Look at this! Take down the wall and here is what St Mary's could be like!' she replied sensibly, 'Yes, but it needs a roof, and if you can't put a bell back up in the tower, they won't let you bring the wall down.' 'How true,' John sighed, but he cut out the photograph and put it in his pocket book.

Later that morning he showed the cutting to his old friend and fellow elder Alec Malcolm, Manager of the British Linen Bank, who was equally impressed. However, he too doubted whether the authorities would ever allow the ruins to be touched.

Undeterred, John showed the photograph to Ian Burns, an Edinburgh surveyor who came to Haddington that same afternoon, to discuss details of a building contract. Was there any chance that it might be possible to re-roof the east end, or was that simply a ridiculous dream? To his surprise, the surveyor foresaw no great technical difficulty in the restoration of the east end, despite its ruinous condition. The real problem would not be the stonework, he said, but the business of gaining consent from the many interested church and government authorities. Elated, John set aside thoughts of a likely bureaucratic nightmare and followed up Ian Burns's suggestion that he speak to (John) Wilson Paterson, a retired Edinburgh architect who had a great deal of experience working on ancient monuments.

Wilson Paterson readily accepted an invitation to visit Haddington, and as he and John walked down to the church he revealed the fact that not only had he been senior architect with the Ministry of Works but he had actually been involved in the insertion of the concrete foundations at St Mary's more than thirty years earlier. John was amazed. Eagerly scanning the arches and pillars with his binoculars, Wilson announced with satisfaction that his tell-tales were still intact. Better still, he was of the opinion that there would be no difficulty at all in putting a new roof on the ruins. Provided it was not heavy, the old walls could easily sustain it. Matching stone, would, of course, have to be found to repair the vast holes in the south wall and replace the missing tracery from the windows, but that could easily be obtained.

As the two men walked quietly among the graves in the ruined choir, John turned to the question of finance. The project would obviously be very expensive. Perhaps the restoration could be done in two phases. In Phase 1 the choir, tower and south transept could be re-roofed, leaving the ruins of the north transept untouched behind a glass wall similar to the one in Coventry Cathedral. The Kirk Session had no money for the work, but if Hilda Nimmo Smith's generous donation could be used for the restoration instead of for a new hall, further funds could then be raised. Should Phase 1 ever materialise, Phase 2 could follow, with the barrier wall being removed and the north transept rebuilt. Excited by the prospect, Wilson was of the opinion that the cost would not be exorbitant, but he too cautioned that consent from all the necessary authorities would be the real hurdle. Indeed, thirteen different bodies were later identified who would have to give their approval before anything could be done and even then there remained the question of funding the operation.

Armed with these expert opinions, John McVie and Alec Malcolm approached the minister with the suggestion that the church hall scheme be adjourned indefinitely in favour of Phase 1 of a grand restoration project. They did not know how the Reverend James Thomson would take it, but in fact he was very enthusiastic, as was the session clerk, James Annand, editor of the *Haddingtonshire Courier*. It was agreed that if John could obtain the consent of all the necessary authorities, Alec would raise the money. They would probably need a further £25,000 in addition to Hilda's £20,000. When they told her what they proposed to do, she was delighted, for she well remembered her father's disappointment when nothing had come of John Christie's intended benefaction. Now, at last, something could be done.

At the monthly Kirk Session meeting on 4 May 1964, the minister invited John McVie to report on the progress of the church hall project. This he did, explaining that a suitable piece of land was now available, and that Alan Reiach the architect was ready to start work. The estimated cost was £40,000. The elders listened with satisfaction but just as they were about to approve the plans, John made his dramatic announcement. He asked them to defer their decision until they had considered an alternative proposal which he was about to make. He would like them to consider the possibility of restoring the choir, tower and south transept of St Mary's.

Forty of the elders were present that evening, and they listened with astonishment as John spoke of the newspaper photograph of St Michael's, Linlithgow, his conversations with Ian Burns and Wilson Paterson, the need for a roof, flooring, new stonework, tracery and heating and, of course, the subsequent increase in space available for church activities once the east end was restored. When he had finished, they burst into animated discussion, some afire with enthusiasm, others vehemently opposed to the idea. Apart from the thought of the expense, they were used to their romantic ruin and some of them felt that they preferred it that way. The church would be utterly spoiled, they believed, if the east end were rebuilt. However, the minister spoke strongly in favour of the new plan, and in the end, possibly out of respect for him, it was unanimously agreed that any decision about the church hall must wait until they had investigated the proposal for the restoration.

A Restoration Committee was set up, with John McVie as its convener and, at a meeting with officials from the Ministry of Works, members learned that the Ministry was likely to give general approval, on condition that the Minister of Works should be asked formally for permission and that the Kirk Session obtain a satisfactory report from a structural engineer on the stability of St Mary's. Wilson Paterson produced a plan for Phase 1. His proposals were incorporated in a report obtained from R.V.M. Liddiard & Burns, chartered surveyors. This proposed that a pitched roof would be placed over the choir and transepts, with sloping roofs to the aisles. The old walls would never support stone vaulting, and so the ceilings would have to be made of wood.

Since the Ministry had previously refused to countenance the construction of a bell chamber, the tower would instead be given a flat roof at a lower level, its upper floors left in their ruinous state. The ground inside the east end would be paved with stone slabs, all the missing stone walls and parapets would be rebuilt, the tracery of the windows would be repaired or replaced, as need be, and leaded glass would be inserted. The north transept would be temporarily screened off, and the east end would be heated, lighted and provided with drainage. The total cost was estimated at £25,455 and the Kirk Session undertook to obtain a structural engineer's report on the pillars from Messrs Leonard and Partners, consulting engineers in Edinburgh. The Kirk Session approved the Liddiard & Burns report and the session clerk wrote to the Ministry of Works seeking formal consent for Phase 1. In order to forestall possible objections, he emphasised in his letter that no extra weight would be placed on the walls, nor was there any intention of putting a bell chamber back on the tower. During Phase 2, the barrier wall and west galleries would be removed and the organ would be relocated in the north transept, with a subsequent rearrangement of the vestry and Session House.

The Ministry of Works considered this application at some length, and in October said that it was prepared to agree to the restoration of St Mary's on four conditions. The General Trustees of the Church of Scotland must reassume responsibility for the whole of the church, the Ministry must be satisfied that the proposals were structurally possible, all plans were to be submitted to it for approval, and the Kirk Session would have to show that they had in their hands a sufficient sum of money to see the work satisfactorily through to its conclusion.

In view of this encouraging response, when the Kirk Session next met, Sir Cameron Badenoch, one of the elders, proposed that Phase 1 of the restoration scheme should go ahead, provided it had the consent of the General Trustees of the Church of Scotland and could be carried out for £25,000. Mention of this large amount of money alarmed some of his listeners, and several senior elders were concerned that the project would take money away from the current Christian Stewardship Campaign. In the end, however, the motion was passed. Later, some of the General Trustees said that it would be a pity not to include the north transept, and the Session agreed to obtain estimates for both Phase 1 and Phase 2. Hilda Nimmo Smith then generously offered to increase her gift from £20,000 to £30,000 and on 6 December 1965, the various tenders for Phase 1 came before the Kirk Session.

The lowest offer for the work came from Messrs Alec Moncrieff, builders in Haddington, who had carried out the restoration of Haddington Town House between 1953 and 1956. They estimated that the work, including the rebuilding of both transepts, would cost £44,000. In addition to Hilda Nimmo Smith's promised £30,000, the finance committee of St Mary's arranged to borrow £14,000 from Barings Bank and there were hopes that a grant from the Pilgrim Trust might be forthcoming. The Presbytery of Haddington and Dunbar gave advance approval to the restoration scheme and the Ecclesiastical Buildings Committee of the General Trustees of the Church of Scotland was also ready to agree, on the understanding that the north transept should be included in Phase 1 and that the Ministry of Works would transfer their guardianship to the General Trustees, who in turn would pass the duty of maintenance to the Kirk Session. Wilson Paterson was optimistic that maintenance costs during the first twenty years would be minimal. The Ministry of Works was prepared to enter into a deed with the General Trustees setting up this new arrangement as soon as they knew that their four conditions had been met.

The Kirk Session heard all these details on 20 December 1965. The elders listened intently and then they gave their opinions. Some remained wary, preferring the financially safer option of a new church hall, others were all for the restoration, and Derick Mills, who would later be session clerk for sixteen years, said that although at first he had been horrified by the scheme, he was now convinced that the church had not been built to be a ruin. Finally, John Munro's motion that Messrs Alec Moncrieff's offer be accepted was unanimously agreed, subject to the receipt of planning permission and formal approval from the Ministry of Works and the General Trustees of the Church of Scotland. It seemed that, after more than four centuries, the east end of St Mary's was to be restored at last.

Members of the Ancient Monuments Board came to inspect the ruins and the Kirk Session prepared to submit their application to East Lothian County Council's Planning Authority. It would then go to the Secretary of State because the east end had ancient monument status. So far everything had gone smoothly, but early in 1966 a worrying problem arose. Ian G. Lindsay, the Edinburgh architect famous for his work on historic buildings such as Iona Abbey and now a government consultant, called on Lord Kilmaine at the offices of the Pilgrim Trust in London on other business. He was surprised when Lord Kilmaine mentioned the St Mary's project, for he had heard nothing about it, and when he saw the architectural drawings he said at once that the proposed wooden panelled ceilings would never do. St Mary's must have a stone vaulted roof to preserve the integrity of the building.

Ian Lindsay and Wilson Paterson later met, and Wilson explained the reason for his choice of a wooden ceiling. The two men were unable to agree and Ian Lindsay died later that year. Before his death, however, he expressed his concerns to the Ancient Monuments Board and when representatives of the Board and the Ministry of Works met Wilson Paterson on 22 April 1966, the Board and Ministry members began by saying that they were not happy with the design of the ceiling. They went on to question other aspects of Wilson's drawings. They were unwilling to accept the use of synthetic or reconstituted stone for the window tracery, they disagreed with the proposed treatment of the tower, they queried the rebuilding of the roof parapets, disliked the glazing of the windows with leaded panes and criticised the proposals for the flooring, the heating system, lighting, sanitation, structural stability and the restoration of missing pinnacles.

Wilson Paterson and the church Restoration Committee were worried and dismayed by these comments. Weeks went by, with urgent correspondence and private discussions, but there was no resolution of the problems. At a meeting in October, the Ancient Monuments Board refused to accept the proposal to erect a flat roof over the choir and insisted on the tower being re-roofed at a high level but there was, however, encouraging progress on what was perhaps the most vital matter. The Board were prepared to withdraw their insistence that traditional materials be used and, in view of the Kirk Session's financial difficulties, they said that they would, after all, be prepared to accept vaulting made of lightweight materials. Eager to proceed, the Kirk Session offered to restore one clerestory window so that the Board could inspect it. The Restoration Committee also agreed to provide drawings for the tower roof at a higher level than previously planned and promised to gather details of how a vaulted ceiling of lightweight materials might be achieved.

The staff of the Ministry of Works were in fact sympathetic to the Restoration Committee's dilemma, and one morning John McVie received from them a mysterious brown paper parcel. When he opened it up, he found that it contained about one and a half feet of glass reinforced polyester, better known as fibreglass. The Ministry had discovered that this material was being used in various English churches. It was light and strong, and could be coloured and shaped as required. There seemed to be no reason why it could not be employed to create ribbing for ceiling vaulting at St Mary's. It weighed so little that it would cause no pressure at all on the walls of the aisles. The problem of the ceiling was solved at last.

Age and ill-health now made it necessary for Wilson Paterson to retire from the project and, with his advice, the church decided to seek an opinion on their plans from Ian G. Lindsay & Partners, whose senior partner was now John Reid. When the firm's reply came in January 1968 it brought grave disappointment. While they agreed that the project was highly commendable, they had been made aware that the East Lothian Planning Officer, the Royal Fine Art Commission and the Scottish Development Department remained unconvinced that the scheme would enhance the beauty and dignity of St Mary's. There was also grave concern that the entire project might fall through for lack of funds. Ian G. Lindsay and Partners believed that the lowest estimate tendered was too low. In their view, the minimum realistic figure would be £60,000. Under the impression that the main purpose of the restoration was to provide additional accommodation, they said that the church would be better to erect an entirely new building, at a cost of £6 to £7 per square foot.

John McVie read this letter to the Kirk Session on 15 January 1968. The elders were horrified at the escalating costs. They deferred any discussion until their next meeting, which took place on 5 February. The letter was then read out once more and one of the elders moved that in view of the report of Ian G. Lindsay and Partners, the restoration scheme should be abandoned. John McVie was absent that evening, on duty at a town council meeting, but Stewart MacPhail, a member of the Restoration Committee, tried to propose that no decision should be taken until further consideration had been given to the situation. His amendment failed to find a seconder. The resolution to cancel the restoration scheme was carried. The Session then appointed a Nimmo Smith Memorial Committee to negotiate the purchase of a suitable site for a new church hall.

Chapter 6

THE LAMP OF LOTHIAN

Members of the Restoration Committee went home that night torn between anger and despair and when they told John McVie what had happened he was appalled. Others, too, felt great dismay when they heard the news, notably the Duchess of Hamilton. Lady Elizabeth Percy, daughter of the 8th Duke of Northumberland, was the wife of Douglas, 14th Duke of Hamilton, the famous boxer and aviator, chief pilot of the first plane to fly over Mount Everest. His ancestral home, Hamilton Palace in Lanarkshire, had been demolished in the 1920's and after service with the Royal Air Force during the Second World War, the Duke decided to look for a pleasant country mansion where he could settle with his wife and their small sons. After viewing various houses throughout Scotland, they finally came upon Lennoxlove.

The former Lethington Tower had passed from the Maitland family with the death of the Duke of Lauderdale in 1682. Alexander, 5th Lord Blantyre purchased it and changed its name to Lennoxlove, as a tribute to his aunt, Frances, Duchess of Richmond and Lennox who had left him the money to buy it. The house remained in his family for the next two centuries, but now it was for sale. The Duke and Duchess purchased it in 1946 and settled there, taking a keen interest in the estate and in the surrounding area. During the 1960s East Lothian, like other parts of the country, was suffering a period of agricultural decline, and many of the older buildings in Haddington were sadly dilapidated. Young people complained that there was nothing for them to do, and church attendance was declining.

The Duke was an elder of Bolton Church, and in 1966 the session clerk sent a letter to all the members of the scattered congregation, describing the falling support for the Church and outlining some of the other problems affecting country communities. The Duke showed the Duchess the letter, and they had long discussions about what could be done to help. Everyone knew about the plans to restore St Mary's. Would it not be possible to refurbish some of the other historic buildings in the town, not as private houses but as a focus for community life? There was Haddington House, the handsome, seventeenth-century building near St Mary's. There was Poldrate Mill, with its cottages. Flour milling had been going on there ever since the fourteenth century, long before the Siege of Haddington, but its future was now in doubt. Some of the young people of the town had said that they would like to make the mill cottages into a folk club, but they lacked the funds to do so. If the buildings could somehow be restored, they could become centres of activity, not just for the townspeople but for everyone from the local area, forming a bridge, as it were, between town and country.

Certainly there could be a folk club, a coffee bar and facilities for crafts, pottery perhaps. The Duchess had even more ambitious ideas, however. There should be concerts, plays and art exhibitions put on by professionals of known reputation and at the same time, outside experts could coach the local young people so that they could take part in musical and dramatic entertainments. By watching and participating, they would not only learn new skills but they would come to appreciate the spiritual values of everyday life. It was an idealistic scheme and it would obviously be a very expensive one but, with the Duke's steadfast support, the Duchess had the energy and experience to make it a reality.

Soon the Duchess had gathered a group of enthusiastic supporters and, seeking a name for the enterprise, they decided to call it 'The Lamp of Lothian'. Haddington's thirteenth-century Franciscan Friary had earned itself that title because it had spread spiritual enlightenment in the Middle Ages. This new organisation would try to do the same in the twentieth century. The Lamp of Lothian Trust was accordingly set up in April 1967, with the Duchess as Chairman and the Earl of Wemyss and Lady Broun Lindsay among the trustees. The Duchess was a formidable fundraiser and she had many influential contacts. The first grant for the Lamp came from the Carnegie Trust UK and soon there were other grants and donations from bodies such as the Scottish Development Department and Haddington Town Council as well as from individuals.

Haddington House was given to the Lamp as its future headquarters, and it was refurbished first. The Trust's offices would be there, and other rooms in the house would be available for visiting artists and guests. There would be a music room for small recitals and art exhibitions as well as the library of the East Lothian Antiquarian and Field Naturalists Society. The Lamp of Lothian intended to purchase Poldrate Mill with its buildings and young men and women from Haddington would help with their conversion. The Bridge Youth Centre accordingly came into being, with a coffee bar and a recreation hall and was opened in 1968. The mill itself would become the Lamp of Lothian Collegiate Centre, a combined arts, community and youth centre with a concert room seating a hundred as well as an art gallery. There were plans to turn the malt house into a workshop for members of the Bridge Youth Club.

The restoration of St Mary's was obviously of central importance to this programme of regeneration, not least because Haddington House and Poldrate Mill lay so close to the church. When the Duchess returned from a holiday in Switzerland to learn that the Kirk Session had abandoned their reconstruction project, she was astonished and deeply dismayed. She called on John McVie to find out what had happened and he made no secret of his anger at the decision. He assured the Duchess, however, that he was not giving up and they were both of the opinion that, if the Kirk Session could be persuaded to reverse their decision, it might then be possible for St Mary's to form a limited partnership with the Lamp of Lothian in order to launch a joint appeal for funds.

It was a delicate situation, for the Lamp could not be seen as interfering in the Kirk Session's decision. The Duchess duly wrote a tactful letter to the minister of St Mary's, expressing sincere regret that the restoration was not going to proceed, and inviting members of the Session to meet the trustees of the Lamp of Lothian to see whether it might be possible to go ahead after all. Perhaps there could be a joint appeal for funds, nation-wide. The minister read out the Duchess's letter at the next Session meeting, and the arguments about the restoration erupted all over again.

Many of the elders were still deeply opposed to the scheme, and yet they were all aware of how successful the Duchess had been in raising money for the Lamp. Some began to think that, with her assistance, the financial implications of restoring St Mary's might not be so dire as they had at first seemed. After a lengthy discussion, one of the elders, Sir Cameron Badenoch, finally moved that the Session's previous decision should be suspended for the time being and that a small committee should be appointed to meet the Lamp of Lothian Trustees. Brushing aside an amendment aimed at reinforcing the previous decision to abandon the restoration, a majority of the elders supported Sir Cameron and so the Session went on to appoint representatives to meet the Lamp Trustees.

The meeting took place at Lennoxlove on 30 April 1968, with the Duchess of Hamilton in the chair. Describing how the Lamp of Lothian Trust had come into being, she explained its aims and reported that £43,000 had already been given in response to its fund-raising campaign. John McVie then outlined the history of the St Mary's restoration project, emphasising that the scheme had already been approved by the Presbytery of Haddington and Dunbar, the General Trustees of the Church of Scotland and, subject to agreement on certain architectural details, by the Ministry of Works. Messrs Ian G. Lindsay & Partners had estimated the likely cost at £60,000 and only

£30,000 was available, but in view of the offer of assistance from the Lamp of Lothian, he had been in touch with the architects again and had that very afternoon received a much more encouraging reply.

An association with the Lamp of Lothian Collegiate Trust would go a long way to clarifying the situation, the senior partner had told him and although John Reid still believed that £60,000 to £80,000 would be required in the way of funding, he saw no problem with a major restoration scheme being undertaken in a series of phases so that the costs could be spread over a period of time. This news was received with satisfaction, and the Lamp Trustees said that they would shortly be launching a new appeal for the restoration of Poldrate Mill and the granary. If this were to be combined with an appeal on behalf of St Mary's, there should be an excellent public response. In the meantime, the Kirk Session might find it useful to contact representatives of other churches which had undergone major restoration, to find out how they had financed their schemes.

The meeting at Lennoxlove had been a success, but even so, when the Kirk Session were told about it, many of the elders remained deeply pessimistic about costs. It was all very well for the Lamp Trustees to speak of grants and appeals, but no one knew how much money they had to find for their own enterprises. One elder thought that £120,000 was a more realistic figure for the restoration of St Mary's rather than the £60,000 mentioned and, even when the work had been done, there would be the maintenance costs of the enlarged church. John McVie said soothingly that the present intention was simply to explore all possibilities. If sufficient funds could not be raised, then the restoration would not go ahead.

Derick Mills, the session clerk, then announced that the Duchess of Hamilton had invited the entire Kirk Session to attend an informal gathering at Lennoxlove. This invitation was accepted, and at 6.30 on the evening of Friday 28 June 1968, a large number of elders made their way to Lennoxlove, where the Lamp of Lothian Trustees and a number of ministers of other churches had assembled, including Dr David Steele of St Michael's Church, Linlithgow. In a relaxed and friendly atmosphere, the elders heard what the Lamp of Lothian was achieving, and were able to chat to those ministers who had experience of similar restoration schemes.

The meeting safely over, the Duchess spoke to many of her friends about St Mary's and Catherine Kennedy, wife of General Sir John Kennedy, made an interesting suggestion. They should try to enlist the support of Yehudi Menuhin, Lady Kennedy said. Yehudi, who was the same age as the Duchess, had made his professional debut when he was only seven and since then he had earned international fame not only for his virtuosity but for his humanitarian concerns. The Duchess had never met the famous violinist, but she well remembered that when she was a young girl her mother had taken her to hear the then child prodigy perform. The Duchess now telephoned Yehudi in London and he agreed to give her twenty minutes at the EMI studios between recording sessions. She flew south at once, and as she said afterwards, 'Long before the twenty minutes were up, I had a new friend, alight with excitement and enthusiasm, proposing a date three weeks ahead to come and play in the church.'

That same evening, on 22 July 1968, the Kirk Session met in St Mary's to discuss the restoration project once more. Torrential rain poured down outside and inside it was almost dark as the elders, seated in the front pews of the nave, entered into a lengthy debate about procedural detail. At last they moved on to the main topic on their agenda, and a letter from the Duchess of Hamilton was read out. In the space of only ten days, she had obtained the promise of £17,000 for St Mary's. There was also a message from the Duke of Hamilton. The Duchess had just telephoned him from London Airport saying that

Yehudi Menuhin would launch a new fundraising initiative by coming to play in St Mary's in three weeks' time.

Hilda Nimmo Smith had promised £30,000, Alec Malcolm had obtained a further £10,000 at least and now, with the £17,000 the Duchess had secured, approximately £50,000 was already available. This was impressive news but many doubts remained for all that and the arguments seemed interminable. John McVie, Alec Malcolm and James Denholm strongly urged that the project should go ahead, while Derick Mills led the opposition. In the end, it was finally agreed by twenty-two votes to sixteen that the restoration should, in principle, proceed. Faithful to his promise, Yehudi Menuhin came to St Mary's on 21 August 1968. The nave was packed and an overflow audience sat in the ruined choir behind the barrier wall, listening as the concert was relayed to them. Not only was this a deeply satisfying musical experience: it was excellent publicity for the restoration project.

Before any work could begin, however, consent was required from a number of important institutions and, while their approval was being sought, the entire building was examined , beginning with the roof. The stone ridging and slating of the nave were found to be in good condition, although the main rafters and timbers beneath were heavily infested with furniture beetle and there had been some wet rot. Nothing structural was required, however, and treatment by Rentokil would be undertaken to rectify the problem. As to the stonework, in general it was in good condition, although of course the damaged areas of wall at the east end would have to be rebuilt and eleven windows would have to be reinstated.

Even with the money promised, fundraising was going to be crucial, and so it was decided to establish a new organisation, the Friends of St Mary's. Its steering committee met for the first time on 20 November 1968, with the Earl of Wemyss as President and John McVie in the chair. The Duchess of Hamilton addressed the meeting. In a clear-sighted report, she urged the committee to remember that although the Lamp of Lothian and the Friends of St Mary's were complementary and indispensable to each other, they were completely different in character. The Friends had a primary role in the field of public relations and, by their very nature, they would involve more and more people in their deliberations.

Naturally, their discussions would take time. The Trust, on the other hand, was a small, close-knit body, legally constituted, holding large capital resources and able to respond rapidly to situations. Having fought its way to financial solvency, the Lamp's primary task was to remain a solvent and effective executive body on whom both the Kirk Session and the bank could rely to handle financial and legal transactions promptly. The Duchess agreed to take on the role of organiser of the new joint appeal, and the Friends of St Mary's was launched at an ecumenical service in the church on 19 January 1969, attended by representatives from the Church of Scotland, the Roman Catholic Church, the Episcopal Church of Scotland and the Society of Friends. The congregation found leaflets in the pews, describing the work of the Lamp and the plan to restore St Mary's.

Obviously a firm of architects well experienced in restoring historical buildings would have to be employed, and Ian G. Lindsay & Partners were appointed. Peter Graham and Partners would act as quantity surveyors and the Edinburgh firm of T. Harley Haddow and Partners would undertake a structural examination of the church walls. On 17 February 1969, Harley Haddow sent in their report, stating that since the 1920s the east gable had gone another half inch off plumb, so that it was now leaning ten and a half inches outwards.

The buttresses on the south wall were half an inch, an inch and a half and seven and a quarter inches out respectively, while the south east column was two and three quarter inches off plumb. Alarming though all this might sound, they pointed out that the underpinning of the 1920s had in fact been successful in arresting all movement in the building and most of the mortar tell-tales placed on the masonry in Wilson Paterson's time were completely unbroken. Although the areas which were badly off plumb might need to be tied back during the reconstruction, the fabric of the building was structurally stable and suitable for reconstruction.

That same day Harley Haddow were officially appointed as structural engineers to the project, and later that month they inspected the tower. They discovered that although the two columns to the east had been underpinned and were in a good state, the north west column required underpinning and so it would be advisable for the south west column to be underpinned as well. They completed their examination of the building in the late spring, recommending that the south-east column in the choir should be taken down and rebuilt. It would not require underpinning, for there was already extensive underpinning in that part of the church.

Two days earlier, the Ecclesiastical Buildings Committee of the General Trustees of the Church of Scotland approved the project, subject to the opinion of their Advisory Committee on Artistic Questions, and that particular sub-committee gave what they termed 'their enthusiastic blessing' on 22 July 1969. The publicity campaign to attract finance intensified that autumn and in September 1969, the Lamp of Lothian staged a musical and theatrical production entitled 'Three Ballads' in St Mary's in September 1969. At Yehudi Menuhin's suggestion, Charles Turner, an American composer with a pioneering approach to teaching musical composition to young people, had proposed producing 'The Ballad of Barnaby' for the Lamp of Lothian.

This was a short opera based on a medieval legend, 'Our Lady's Juggler'. It had a text by W.H. Auden the poet, the music had been composed by Charles Turner's young pupils and Rhoda Levine was choreographer. To give local relevance to the performance, two Scottish ballads were added to the evening's entertainment, 'True Thomas', set to music by a nineteen-year-old from East Lothian and 'The Four Maries' by a sixteen-year-old pupil of Knox Academy, Haddington. Fifty young people from East Lothian made up the cast of 'Three Ballads', spending every spare minute rehearsing for five weeks before their successful performance.

The following month, on 15 October 1969, another musical entertainment took place in St Mary's. 'The Lamp of Licht' was devised to celebrate the first three years of the Lamp of Lothian Centre. Lennox Milne and Tom Fleming, the distinguished Scottish actors who were both working with the Lamp, were the speakers, while Joan Dickson the cellist and her sister Hester, the pianist, Duncan Robertson, the tenor, choirs from the local churches, the cast of 'Three Ballads' and members of the Roman Catholic Community of Sancta Maria, Nunraw provided the music. Queen Elizabeth The Queen Mother was present that evening, for she had agreed to become the Royal Patron of the Friends of the church and, of course, her visit attracted a good deal of welcome attention in the press. More and more people were becoming aware of the plans to restore St Mary's.

Chapter 7

THE RESTORATION OF ST MARY'S

Throughout the early months of 1970, the Restoration Committee eagerly awaited the consent they needed to go ahead with their plans. Both the minister, the Reverend James Thomson, and his assistant John Harris left St Mary's at the end of January 1970, but the Very Reverend Dr Nevile Davidson was appointed interim moderator until a new minister could be selected. A former Moderator of the General Assembly of the Church of Scotland, Dr Davidson was a leading figure in the Church and he strongly supported the restoration scheme. On 2 February 1970 East Lothian County Council gave planning permission, subject to various conditions and by the end of April the Ministry of Works architect, George Hay, had accepted the plans subject to twelve minor points being agreed. John Reid incorporated these amendments in his programme, which was approved by the Restoration Committee on 30 June 1970. The Kirk Session then gave their consent.

Frank Tindall, the County Planning Officer, had asked the Royal Fine Art Commission for their comments, and they too now gave their approval. The planning authority itself would meet on 24 August. By now the estimated cost of restoring the east end of the church had risen to £103,500. The rebuilding of the walls was the most expensive item, at over £31,000, the roofing would cost over £19,000 and the charge for the fibreglass ceilings would be £14,320. Arrangements were made to convey responsibility for the ruins from the Ministry of Works to the Church of Scotland Trustees. The Lauderdale Aisle would, however, continue to be under the guardianship of the Ministry, while the Earl of Lauderdale and his family remained responsible for the vaults beneath the aisle. An application for planning consent was dispatched to East Lothian County Council and a petition for a building warrant was submitted to Haddington Dean of Guild Court. That autumn, there was great activity as firms were approached and invited to tender for the work.

One of the priorities was to identify stone which would match the red Garvald sandstone of the existing church. Locharbriggs Quarries, Dumfries were asked what their stone was like and Natural Stone Quarries of Durham sent up two samples of St Bees red stone for the tracery of the windows. John Reid worried that it was too light in colour. He sent a small sample of the St Mary's stone to Durham, and the firm assured him that their St Bees stone would weather to a suitable shade. Natural Stone Quarries also tendered for the stone floor paving. In October, firms in Lowestoft, Grimsby, Somerset and Bradford were consulted about fibreglass for the vaulted ceilings. Laminators (Lowestoft) Limited, a boat-building firm, advised using a fibreglass coated with a fire retardant gell and sent in their estimate.

The organ would have to be dismantled and removed, and Rushworth & Dreaper Ltd, organ builders, who regularly tuned the instrument, were asked how much that would cost. John Reid was then approached with the interesting offer of a stained glass window. The Council for the Care of Churches explained that the window had been designed in 1877 by Edward Burne-Jones, the noted pre-Raphaelite artist. At the top was the Crucifixion, the cross flanked by the Virgin Mary and St John, and beneath were six scenes from the life of Christ. Originally installed in St Michael's Church, Torquay, the window had been saved when that church was demolished, because it was a fine example of the work of Burne-Jones. The Victoria and Albert Museum in London had agreed to store it and for the past thirty years it had been reposing in crates in the Museum. Perhaps St Mary's would like to have it. John Reid replied, expressing cautious enthusiasm. Everything would depend upon whether its measurements matched a window in St Mary's and then there was the question of transport costs. The expense might prove too great. On a more mundane note, arrangements were in hand to install an electric service lift for the use of the

builders and joiners, and lengthy discussions began about the design and siting of the new boiler.

Meanwhile, the Duchess of Hamilton was pressing ahead with her fund-raising activities. Towards the end of 1970, she was able to report that an anonymous donor had offered to give £30,000 by means of a seven year covenant, for the benefit of the restoration of St Mary's and the activities of the Lamp of Lothian Trust. As more and more donations and covenants flowed in, a special Joint Financial Co-ordinating Committee was set up, consisting of the Duchess, the honorary treasurers of the Kirk Session, the Lamp of Lothian and the Friends of St Mary's, along with John Porter, Manager of the British Linen Bank. In March 1971 the Duchess went to London to see the Pilgrim Trust.

On 12 April the Dean of Guild Court in Haddington issued the vital building warrant. Work on St Mary's could begin. The Kirk Session met for the first time in Haddington House on 17 May and chose as their new minister the Reverend James Riach. At that same meeting, the Restoration Committee was at last able to report that their plans had been approved not only by all the relevant official bodies but by the Secretary of State for Scotland. Now that the various tenders had come in, Peter Graham & Partners, chartered quantity surveyors, estimated that the total cost of the work would be £130,604.77. The sum of £107,250 had been either raised or promised.

Because of the shortfall, the elders decided to leave part of the work until a second phase. During Phase 1 the shell of the east end would be restored but the interior refurbishment would have to wait until Phase 2. The removal of the organ gallery, attention to the floors, provision of internal doors, the fibreglass vaulted ceilings, heating, plumbing and ventilation, electrical services and paintwork could be undertaken only when the necessary funding had been secured. Even at this stage, some of the elders were still doubtful about the whole idea, but after a discussion lasting for three hours, they agreed unanimously to go ahead. Indeed, after the formal part of the meeting was over, more than a dozen of those who had previously been strongly opposed came and told John McVie that they would give their wholehearted support.

(*left*) St Mary's in August 1971, with the ruined east end visible on the left. (*Duncan Brash*)

(*below*) The Tower of St Mary's, seen from the east window, through scaffolding. August 1971. (*Duncan Brash*)

On 17 June the Pilgrim Trust announced that they were granting £5,000 to St Mary's. Messrs Alexander Hall and Son's men started work on the site on 19 July 1971. John McVie later recalled how the area to the north of the nave took on the look of a hutted camp, with daily arrivals of steel, timber, stones and other materials, while scaffolding was erected and the stone masons began their work. John Reid's colleague Crichton Lang was deeply impressed when he visited the site that first day. He knew how many people had serious doubts about the entire project and he felt an awesome sense of responsibility as he witnessed the hustle and bustle and noise. It was going to be a huge undertaking.

The builders would begin by excavating the ground so that a new concrete floor could be laid, incorporating ducts for the heating system. Their first task was therefore to remove the gravestones from the ruins. The architects gave them a drawing, showing the position of all the stones and Hall's men were instructed to lift each stone, number it to correspond with the drawing, and put it carefully aside. When the new paving was laid, the gravestones would be set into it, each in its original position. The stones were duly removed and soon lorries carrying away earth dug from the floor began to rumble through the town. As the digging went on, large quantities of human bones were found, from the medieval cemetery, and these were carefully re-interred in a pit beneath what would become the new floor.

In August, work began on underpinning the two pillars at the crossing. T. Harley Haddow and Partners had to excavate the base of each pillar, jack it up, brace it and then concrete in the jacks so that it was held on steel supports while a new concrete foundation sixteen feet square and four feet deep was inserted. It was a nerve-wracking operation, but everything went smoothly and by 26 October 1971, the underpinning was complete. Meanwhile, the architects were wrestling with the problem of finding enough stone to repair the walls. Fortunately the Caledonian Station in Edinburgh was being demolished, as were St James's Square and the Chancelot Flour Mills in the city and as early as May 1971 three loads of dressed red ashlar stone from the redundant station had arrived at the church.

In the months that followed, however, maintaining the supply of stone was to be one of the greatest difficulties. It was relatively easy to find rubble stone, but the red and the yellowish white sandstone were much harder to locate. Even the Chancelot Mill stone was not ideal, for it arrived in large pieces which required a great deal of working and dressing on site before it could be used. On one occasion a near crisis was averted when a newly-qualified architect working on the project returned to his office and announced triumphantly that he had bought a railway bridge. He had come upon it in Duns as it was being demolished, and had realised that the stone was just right. In the end 1,500 tons of stone from 140 different sites all over the east of Scotland were employed before the walls were finally finished some thirteen months after work had begun.

Apart from stone for the walls, red stone was also required for the missing tracery of the windows, and it was decided that the St Bees stone offered by Natural Stone Quarries was indeed suitable. The firm would do all the work necessary on the clerestory windows, fitting glazing grooves, replacing tracery and mullions and undertaking other small repairs. They would also supply the stone for the other windows, and would fit their glazing grooves, but Hall's would build the mullions and tracery. Plain, leaded glass would then be inserted by a firm of glaziers and James Thow, Leith Glazing and CDW were each asked to submit estimates. Work on the windows began in September 1971 and was to continue until October 1972.

By October 1971, the walls were rising rapidly and Crichton Lang had to decide exactly how roof and walls would meet. Obviously there were no written records of how the church had orginally been put together, but those working in St Mary's had come to realise that the techniques used in the twentieth century were little different from those of the Middle Ages, apart from the fact that modern scaffolding was made of steel rather than of wood. This gave the masons the distinct sensation that their medieval predecessors were looking over their shoulders to make sure that the job was being done properly. Everyone was therefore determined that as much of the work as possible should be true to the intentions of the original builders.

Standing outside the church and gazing upwards, Crichton Lang could see what looked like a cornice, the continuous horizontal moulding found at the top of a wall. When,

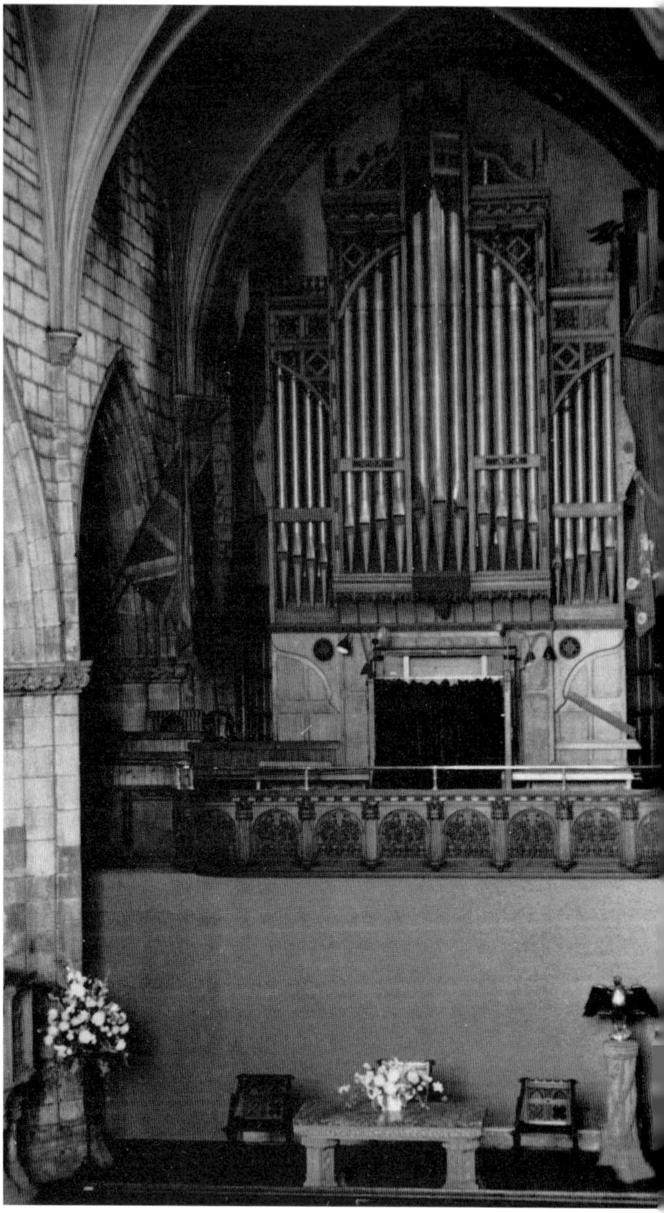

however, he climbed up the scaffolding inside one day and stood for a long time, gazing around him, he had a strange sensation. 'I have never, ever experienced anything like it', he remembered afterwards, 'but I was taken by the arm, I felt a presence beside me, beyond any shadow of doubt, and I was propelled along the scaffold to the corner by the north transept and there in front of me was one stone.' That stone meant that there had not been a cornice at all, but a series of corbels or stone brackets. In that moment, he saw how he should proceed.

(left) The organ against the barrier wall, February 1972. (*Duncan Brash*)

(below) A mason at work at St Mary's, March 1972. (*Duncan Brash)*

(bottom) Hilda Nimmo Smith removes the first stone from the barrier wall, watched by (l to r) the Reverend James Riach, Provost Fraser Spowage and John McVie, 17 March, 1972.(*East Lothian Courier*)

Work on the roof of the choir began the following month. Barnet and Morton of Kirkcaldy erected the steel trusses and purlins which would form the new roof, and the rafters were put up. Plumbers then installed the rainwater drainage system, after which the slaters got to work. Similar roofs were put on the south transept, the tower, and finally, the north transept. By the end of February 1972, building work on the external walls of choir and transepts was almost finished, and the time was fast approaching when the great barrier wall separating choir from nave could be removed. Before that could happen, however, the organ and organ gallery which stood against it would have to be dismantled.

Dr Louis Rusack, himself a keen organist, was appointed to form an organ sub-committee to liaise with the architects and organ builders, and at the beginning of March 1972 the organ was taken apart and stored in the gallery of Newton Port Church Hall. That done, a simple but exciting ceremony took place at noon on 17 March. The builders had loosened a suitable stone in the barrier wall and John McVie formally invited Hilda Nimmo Smith to remove it. Watched by a gathering which included the Duchess of Hamilton, Dr Nevile Davidson, the Restoration Committee, John Reid and Crichton Lang, the architects, Hilda took the hammer and chisel, carefully freed the heavy stone and, with the help of the Reverend James Riach, Fraser Spowage the provost of Haddington and John McVie, lifted it from its position.

The masons went to work and down came the rubble wall. For the first time since the 1560s, the full extent of the church was revealed. However, because the nave was going to continue in use as the parish church during the remainder of the restoration work, it was not possible to leave the choir and crossing open, and so a wire reinforced polythene screen was put up where the barrier wall had been, and sealed to keep out the dust. Phase 1 was now complete, and that autumn the Edinburgh artist Maxwell Allan was invited to

design an inscription for a slab to be laid at the crossing, commemorating the removal of the first stone from the barrier wall. In view of their close association with the project, Natural Stone Quarries generously offered to donate the £250 slab.

Phase 2 was due to start before the beginning of July 1972, but how was it to be funded? Dr Nevile Davidson was now Chairman of the Friends of St Mary's, and membership was growing steadily. In a report on 7 July 1972, the Duchess of Hamilton announced that, together, the Kirk Session, the Lamp of Lothian Trust and the Friends of St Mary's had since the previous September raised £30,000 in donations and £55,000 in loans, the latter including £15,000 from East Lothian County Council, £10,000 from Mr Mungo Campbell, £20,000 from Lord Bute and £10,000 from the Research for Truth Foundation. This had been just enough to finance the contract for Phase 1.

In order to help pay off the loans, the Kirk Session decided to sell the four silver communion cups made for the church by Patrick Borthwick in 1645. A replica set had been obtained in 1902, and since then the originals had been kept in the safety of a Bank of Scotland vault. There remained, however, the pressing question of how

best to raise the money for Phase 2. Messrs Hooker, Craigmyle, Scotland Ltd, a firm of professional fund-raisers, had been consulted, and with their advice it was decided to launch a new fund-raising campaign in October, with leaflets, events and volunteer groups who would target both individuals and organisations likely to take an interest.

Having listened to the Duchess's plans, the Kirk Session were confident that the necessary finance would be forthcoming and Phase 2 began. Natural Stone Quarries would supply 685 square yards of Whitehaven mottled paving, two inches thick, for the new floor, J.T.L. Parkinson-Twaddle

(left) The barrier wall comes down and the north transept goes up, April 1972. (*Duncan Brash*)

(centre) The transept walls, three feet thick, being rebuilt, April 1972. (*Duncan Brash*)

(right) The tracery of the north transept window in position, May 1972. (*Duncan Brash*)

Ltd were employed to instal the heating, different types of lighting were being discussed, and William Allan Smith and Company Limited, Edinburgh were given the contract for the electrical work. Laminators (Lowestoft) had been chosen to provide the fibreglass ceilings, and they had been scheduled to start on 17 June, finishing by 13 September. Unfortunately, there was a delay, and because of problems in the building industry, Hall's masons had taken part in a series of strikes in June, July and August, making it impossible for work on the ceilings to begin. When Laminators' workmen did arrive on 2 October, they could do nothing, of course, as the church had been cleared for an important concert.

On 1 October the new appeal for funds had begun with an ecumenical service and on 3 October Yehudi Menuhin played once more in St Mary's. Now a Patron of the Friends, he brought his sister Hepzibah, a famous pianist, with him and they were able to perform in the re-roofed choir. During the first part of October, an exhibition was held in Poldrate Mill, tracing the history of the restoration, and on 8 October there was a programme of music and poetry in the church, 'Singular Solace', similar to the Lamp of Licht concert held three years earlier. After 'Singular Solace', Laminators' ceiling fixers should have been able to begin work, but when scaffolding was erected for them, they declared it to be unsafe. Crichton Lang authorised a further £600 to be spent on modifying it and it was dismantled on 9 October. New scaffolding towers were put up in the choir two days later, allowing no fewer than twelve ceiling fixers to operate at any one time.

Laminators' men were to put up simulated stone ribs, each measuring approximately twelve by eight inches, made in four ounces per square foot chopped strand mat glass, impregnated with polyester resin which complied with fire retardancy conditions. The simulated plaster infill spandrels, in other words, the triangular white panels between the arched ribs, arrived at the church in rolls. In all, there would be some 2000 linear feet of stone ribs, 9000 square feet of spandrels and twenty nine ceiling bosses of various designs. When they began putting up the ceilings of the first bay of the choir, the fixers encountered an unexpected difficulty. They discovered that the main ribs they were using had been manufactured to the wrong curvature, and so they had to cut and re-bond them on site. This meant further delay, and of course they had to stop work whenever there was a wedding or some other function in the nave.

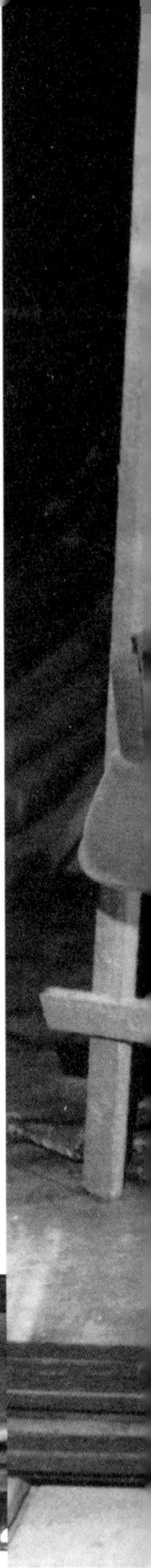

(right) Workmen positioning one of the fibre glass ribs of the ceiling, November 1972. (*Duncan Brash*)

(below) The Duchess of Hamilton with Yehudi and Hepzibah Menuhin at St Mary's, for the concert on 3 October 1972. (*Duncan Brash*)

When they reached the south transept, there was another problem, Eleven ribs had to be fitted on to a corbel stone and this proved so difficult that the fixers in the end threw down their tools and declared that it could not be done. Crichton Lang promptly took them to St Giles Cathedral in Edinburgh, where they lay down on their backs on the pews and stared at the double ribbing above them until they saw how to proceed. Often things were not precisely symmetrical in the Middle Ages, but were adjusted to make them look as if they were so. This was what would have to be done at St Mary's. Back they went to work, while the builders' men complained bitterly that their progress in laying the stone paving was being delayed by the fact that Laminators' scaffolding was occupying the space in the choir aisles where they needed to work. This problem was solved by raising the scaffolding legs so that the men could complete their paving beneath it.

Undaunted, the architects and contractors worked on. Dr Rusack and his sub-committee began to investigate the cost of rebuilding and re-siting their dismantled organ and William Minay, the well-known organist of St Cuthbert's Church in Edinburgh, drew up a specification for it. Laminators were still putting up their fibreglass ribs and spandrels, and Formasons of Edinburgh meanwhile estimated for cleaning the interior stonework of the east end. Having stood open to the skies for more than four centuries, it was badly in need of attention. Formasons would use a high-pressure water jet, working overtime if need be to suit the progress of the ceiling fixers. The four silver communion cups had by now been sent to Sotheby's in London, and on 30 November 1972 John and Lindsaye McVie went along to the Auction Rooms for the sale to find the Duke and Duchess of Hamilton already there. They all waited patiently for Lots 113 and 114 to come under the hammer, and were highly gratified when the first pair of cups was sold for £20,000 and the second pair went for £21,000.

By that time, work on the tower was almost finished. Flooring had been put in, it had been re-roofed, and the lighting was going in. New lighting had already been installed in the rest of the church, and the new heating system was almost complete. By the beginning of 1973, Charles Henshaw & Sons Ltd, architectural metalworkers were quoting for brass door furniture, the placing of radiators was under discussion and Watson and Ryman Limited were estimating for a supply of stacking chairs. It had finally been confirmed that the stained glass window from St Michael's, Torquay, was indeed almost an exact match for one of the windows in the south transept. Only a slight extension of the

tops of the panels would be needed to make it fit. The Earl of Wemyss generously donated the money necessary to instal it in the window which had been restored in 1892 at his great-grandfather's expense.

By now, Dr Rusack and his Organ Committee had completed lengthy discussions with several firms of organ builders, but they had reached the reluctant conclusion that there was not enough money available to rebuild the existing organ in the foreseeable future. The congregation appeared to be reasonably happy with the piano which had replaced the organ in the church, Dr Rusack and the committee were conscious that it was only an interim measure and they decided to see if any other church was trying to dispose of its organ. Unfortunately, although they visited various churches throughout Scotland and the north of England, they were unable to find anything suitable.

Instead, they resolved to buy a small organ which could be sold again when their own original instrument was reinstated. At Langside Church in Galashiels they heard a small Walker Positif C organ, a type highly recommended by both William Minay and by the organists of York Minster and Liverpool and Blackburn Cathedrals. J.W.Walker and Sons agreed to supply and erect the new organ at a special price of £3650. St Mary's had no money set aside for this, but three dozen members of the congregation came to the rescue each agreeing to give as an interest free loan, never likely to be repaid. The new instrument was duly delivered to St Mary's on 26 March 1973.

The Wemyss Memorial Window, by Burne-Jones. (*Duncan Brash*)

Chapter 8

BELLS FOR THE MILLENNIUM

A week earlier, on 19 March 1973, a significant ceremony had taken place in the choir beside the polythene screen. Hilda Nimmo Smith was there, along with members of the Restoration Committee and representatives of the Friends of St Mary's and the Lamp of Lothian, but the Duchess of Hamilton was absent, for she had to be in Edinburgh that afternoon with the Duke, who was undergoing an operation. John Reid made a short speech, produced a Certificate of Completion and formally delivered to the church the custody and future responsibility for the restored fabric of the choir and transepts.

Mr Shearer, senior foreman with Alexander Hall and Son, presented the keys of the new doors of the north and south transepts to John McVie, who received them on behalf of the Kirk Session. Exactly nine years had passed since John had opened his *Scotsman* at breakfast time, seen the photograph of St Michael's, Linlithgow and been inspired with the idea of somehow achieving the restoration of St Mary's. There had been enormous difficulties along the way but, with energy and determination, these had been overcome. Many years later, Crichton Lang recalled how he and others had felt a special atmosphere in the church throughout the reconstruction, and had become convinced that the Holy Spirit was driving them on.

The last communion service held in the nave, 8 April 1973. (*Duncan Brash*)

The very day after the completion ceremony, the Duke of Hamilton died suddenly. Bereft of his loving support, his indomitable Duchess nonetheless continued her efforts, and on 12 July 1973 Her Majesty The Queen and Prince Philip visited Haddington to see all that had been achieved. They went first to St Mary's, where they were welcomed by the Earl of Wemyss, Lord Lieutenant of East Lothian. They met Provost Spowage in his robes of office and John McVie in wig and gown, as town clerk, along with Mrs Spowage and Mrs McVie and then they moved into the churchyard where the Duchess of Hamilton, the Very Reverend Dr and Mrs Davidson and the minister, the Reverend James Riach, and his wife were waiting.

The minister conducted the royal party to the west door, pointing out the marks of sixteenth-century bullets and cannon balls on the south wall. Inside, Derick Mills the session clerk, Joe Henderson the beadle and ten members of the Restoration Committee were presented: Stewart MacPhail, Bill Ferguson, Tommy Wood, Alec McRobbie, David Miller, Bill Smith, John Cairns, Duncan Robertson, John Porter and Dr Louis Rusack. John McVie escorted The Queen and Prince Philip round the east end of the church and in the choir they met Hilda Nimmo Smith. Smartly dressed in a checked coat and light-coloured beret, Hilda described how her father had always hoped to see St Mary's restored and The Queen congratulated her on her outstanding generosity. The Queen and the Prince then viewed photographs taken by Duncan Brash during the course of the restoration and admired the Wemyss Memorial Window, before finally leaving for Haddington House, their visit a satisfying culmination of all the years of planning, persuasion and hard work.

The royal visit safely accomplished, volunteers from the congregation, led by Tommy Wood, Bill Smith and Joe Henderson, set about moving the pews. There was still work to be done in the nave. The polythene screen would therefore stay

(top) HM The Queen speaks to Hilda Nimmo Smith during the royal visit to St Mary's on 12 July 1973. (*East Lothian Courier*)

(above) John McVie escorts HM The Queen to see the Wemyss Memorial Window, 12 July 1973. (*East Lothian Courier*)

The stone with the angels holding Haddington's crest
(above) – before repair (*Source unidentified*)
(right) – after repair (*Duncan Brash*)

in place for the time being and services would be held in the choir. Tommy Wood and his colleagues took the old pews from the nave and cut them to size to fit into the new space. The parishioners then sat with their backs to the east window, facing the screen. It was hardly the most beautiful sight in the world, but it was a sign that progress was continuing and as well as looking directly at the minister, people could see the splendid Wemyss Memorial Window. The first service to be held in the choir for more than four centuries took place on 2 September 1973 and the first Communion there was held the following month.

The corners of the north and south aisles at the east end of the choir were being transformed into two new chapels for private prayer. The Columba Chapel was called after the famous saint who settled in Iona in the sixth century, and the Lady Chapel was named for the Virgin Mary, to whom the church was dedicated. On 3 August 1973, John McVie received a letter from the Duchess of Hamilton explaining that she had been approached by two anonymous donors, one an American, offering to pay for a tapestry to be hung in each of these chapels. The tapestries were commissioned from the famous Dovecote Studios in Edinburgh, and created by Archibald Brennan after consultations with the Duchess, the Reverend James Riach, John Reid and representatives of the Restoration Committee.

The tapestry for the Lady Aisle, in the north east corner, is in shades of grey, brown and blue, representing the colours of the East Lothian coast, and it incorporates the words spoken by the Virgin Mary when the angel told her that she would give birth to the Son of God: 'Be it done unto me according to Thy Word'. The Columba Aisle tapestry is red, brown and purple, symbolising the agricultural landscape of East Lothian, and it has the woven words, 'Come Holy Spirit'. The church was further beautified by a poignant reminder of its medieval past. During excavations near the north transept in connection with drainage, workmen had dug up four or five pieces of a medieval stone which had been buried well below surface. James Fairbairn, a member of the congregation who was a master mason, skilfully reassembled the fragments, putting together two angels holding between them a shield with the Haddington goat on its hind legs, nibbling the tree of grapes. It was then placed on the east wall.

In 1974, St Mary's set up a Congregational Board with its own Fabric Committee to look after the building and on 22 May the Budgeting Committee met in Haddington House to assess the current financial situation. Colin Campbell was able to report that the interest free loan of £7000 granted by the General Trustees of the Church of Scotland did not have to be repaid for another two years, and the loan of £15,000 was not due for repayment until 1980. However, apart from raising these sums, St Mary's would have to find money for what would become Phase 3 of the restoration. John McVie outlined the priorities. Not only would the new heating system in the choir have to be extended to the nave, but the decorative schemes of choir and nave would have to be integrated. The nave's wooden block floor was in need of repair, it would have to be cleaned and the ceiling must be painted to match as closely as possible the ceiling of the choir.

Apart from those improvements, the porch at the west end would have to be altered. Not only was it a fire hazard, but members of the congregation entering that way had to negotiate dangerous steps. When he heard about the problem with the porch, Crichton Lang generously offered to plan a new entrance foyer without charging a fee. He designed a much safer set of steps with a handrail, leading to a spacious foyer on the same level as the nave, and with two side rooms which later became a bookstall and kitchen. Haddington Town Council were hoping to make a grant of £5,000 to cover the cost of work on the heating, the nave floor and the ceiling in Phase 3, and were waiting for approval from the Scottish Office.

Meanwhile the Friends of St Mary's and the Lamp of Lothian were continuing their efforts. The previous October the regimental band, herald trumpeters and pipers of the 1st Battalion of the Royal Scots had given a rousing performance in the church, and the Lamp's celebrated patron Yehudi Menuhin returned whenever his engagements brought him to Scotland. In all, he was to play in St Mary's seven times, his visits ending only with his death in 1999. Looking ahead to the time when all the work would finally be completed, the Council of Friends decided on 30 July 1974 to set up a group of volunteers who would welcome visitors to the church and guide them round. Drawn from the Friends and the congregation, these guides would be known as Guardians of St Mary's.

It was all very well to plan for the future, but the actual work on the nave could not begin until more money had been raised, and there were further delays when pipes for the new nave heating system were not delivered on time. However, work on Phase 3 finally began in the spring of 1975. The pipes arrived at the beginning of March and the heating contractor, Parkinson-Twaddle Ltd of Edinburgh, installed the new system, which was later extended by Jimmy Davie, a Haddington plumber. JL Floor Finishing Company Limited repaired the wooden area of flooring in the nave. Several years earlier it had been decided that the Victorian communion table should be moved to the east end of the church and replaced by a new table standing on a central dais beneath the crossing. Tommy Wood with joiners and cabinetmakers from the congregation made the circular wooden dais in four sections. It was then put in position and covered with a blue carpet.

The summer of 1975 brought exciting recognition for all the work that had been done in the church when St Mary's was given a European Architectural Heritage Award. The burgh of Haddington received a separate award, and in his letter supporting that application, Frank Tindall, the East Lothian Planning Officer, pointed out that all but eleven of 129 buildings of architectural or historic interest in the town now enjoyed a secure future. Thanks to the efforts of the Lamp of Lothian Trust no less than £400,000 had been raised. Frank, once the implacable opponent of the restoration of St Mary's, added, 'The climax of this continuous conservation process was a restoration of the choir and transept of the great parish church of St Mary's.' As the months had passed and he had seen what was being done, his doubts had been replaced by enthusiastic admiration.

Queen Elizabeth The Queen Mother, Royal Patron of the Friends of St Mary's for the past six years, presented the award certificate at a ceremony in St Cecilia's Hall, Edinburgh on 24 June 1975. Less than a month later, there was an alarming moment when two areas of the reconstructed part of the church seemed to be showing signs of movement. The mullions of the north transept window appeared to be splitting and the existing crack on the west side of the north transept, over the first arch to the north nave aisle, looked as though it were widening. James Wren, one of the partners of T. Harley Haddow & Partners, examined both window and arch, but reached the reassuring conclusion that there was no cause for concern.

Having installed the circular dais beneath the crossing, the Restoration Committee turned their attention to the pulpit. Everyone agreed that it was in the wrong place but since it was made of stone, with a marble foundation, it was far too heavy to move. After great controversy, it was finally agreed that it should stay where it was. It could be used when there was a small congregation or a private function, but otherwise the minister would preach from a smaller wooden pulpit, set with its back to the north east pillar of the tower. In June 1976 T. Harley Haddow and Partners were asked to estimate for the new pulpit.

After that, the final contractor to be employed on Phase 3 was the firm of Campbell & Smith (Construction) Co. Limited of Ormiston, who created the new entrance area at the west door. That done, the polythene screen was removed and St Mary's was restored to its medieval proportions at last. The sturdy columns stood firmly on their strengthened foundations, the repaired walls soared upwards to the amazing fibreglass ceiling, and the spring sunshine shone through the clear leaded panes of the reconstructed windows. When the first service for four hundred years was held in the entire church on 17 April 1977, the congregation sat once more in the nave, their backs to the west door, looking right along past the place where the barrier wall had stood, past the transepts and the choir to the very east end of the church.

The nave itself required further attention in 1984, when its roof, stonework, windows and lightening conductors were found to be in need of repair. Crichton Lang arranged for the minister, the Reverend Alastair Macdonell, and Robin Salvesen, Chairman of the Congregational Board, to meet the Historic Buildings Council and explain the problems involved. The cost of the further repairs was estimated at £45,000 and in February 1984 the Council agreed to make a grant of £25,000 towards the work, which was then carried out. That same year, the congregation set up a Promotion and Management Committee to oversee the arrangements for the thousands of visitors who come to the church.

Not long afterwards, Christine Milligan became the first paid Administrator, organising the team of volunteers who welcome visitors and run the small shop. Between eighty and 130 people from all denominations now work together in St Mary's, which is open each day from Easter to October. At noon on weekdays, a short service is conducted by a representative from one of the various denominations. Past opposition to the restoration has long since been forgotten, and the church funds have gone from strength to strength. The money earned as a result of the Promotion and Management Committee's endeavours goes direct to the Fabric Fund, and in 1985 the church funds as a whole stood at £42,498. By 1999, this total would reach £245,848.

When the nave repairs had been completed, there remained a few finishing touches still to be

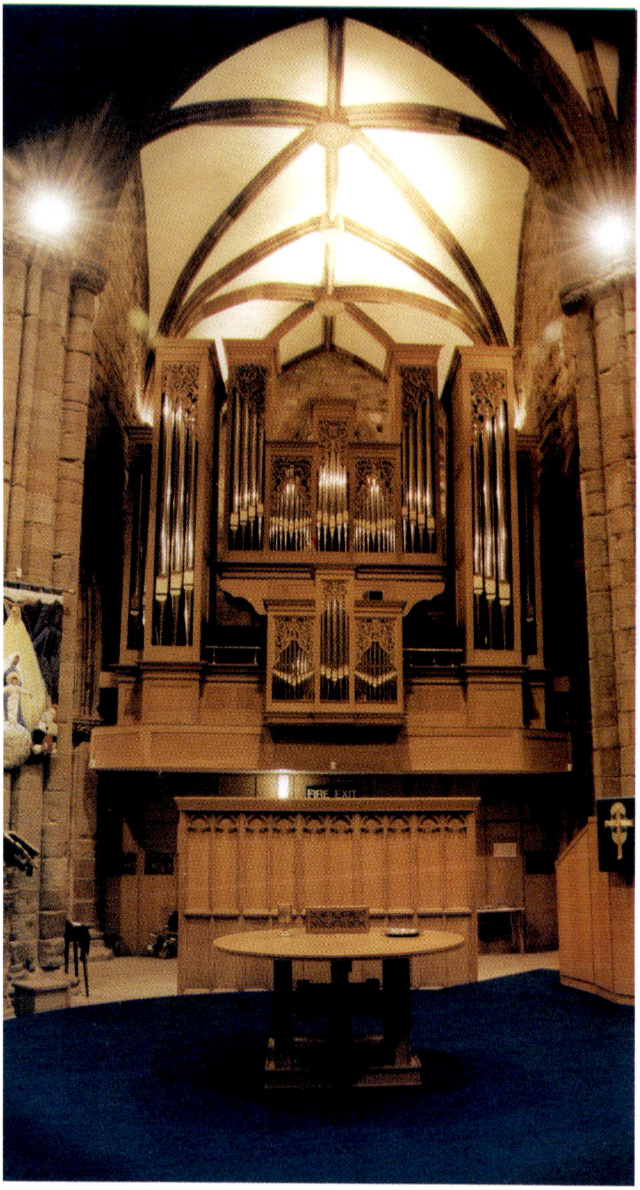

made. The question of the organ, for example, was as yet unresolved. The small Walker instrument was adequate for services, but a church the size of St Mary's deserved something much more impressive, all the more so since it had in recent years become famous for its concerts. An entirely new organ still seemed out of reach because its construction was liable to be prohibitively expensive. One day in the late 1980s, however, a BBC engineer arrived to check the acoustics in preparation for a recording. Realising that the organ needed to be tuned before the broadcast, the BBC recommended Neil Richerby, an organ builder at Oldhamstocks, just a few miles away.

Dr Rusack contacted Neil and learned that he had studied the organ at the Royal Northern College of Music in Manchester and served his apprenticeship with Church & Co in Northumberland. After working in London and Germany, Neil built and designed organs in Canada before settling in an old schoolhouse in Oldhamstocks in 1983. Transforming the old school into his workshop, he set up in business under the name Lammermuir Pipe Organs. Not only did he agree to tune the small Walker organ. He told Dr Rusack that he could build a completely new organ for the north transept of St Mary's at a cost of £50,000.

This seemed almost too good to be true. Professor Peter Williams, formerly of Edinburgh University but by now occupying the Arts and Sciences Distinguished Chair at Duke University in North Carolina, recommended Neil with great enthusiasm, and a special appeal for organ funds was launched. One gift of £20,000 came from the Scottish Post Office Board as part of its support for 'The Year of the Bible', as 1988 had been designated. Gifts and bequests flowed in, and by the spring of 1990, the organ was ready. It is of traditional design, the three departments clearly visible, the large centre light oak case flanked on either side by the pedal towers, the choir organ overhanging the gallery front. On 27 May 1990, Peter Williams flew over to perform the inaugural recital, playing music by Bach, Sir Hubert Parry, John Stanley and Samuel Sebastian Wesley. That same year, a new round communion table of simple but elegant design was installed on the blue dais and in 1993 the musical reputation of the church was further enhanced with the appointment of a new minister, the Reverend Clifford Hughes, himself a well-known singer with a singularly beautiful tenor voice.

One final addition was needed to perfect the restoration of St Mary's. Ever since 1548 the church tower had been bereft of its bells. There was no possibility of putting back the original *(left)* The new Lammermuir Pipe Organ, installed in St Mary's in 1990. (*Duncan Brash*)

(below) The Reverend Clifford Hughes welcomes Cardinal Thomas Winning to St Mary's, 1992. (*T. Scott Roxburgh*)

three which the English had carried away. These had been allegedly given to Durham Cathedral, but although the Dean of the Cathedral had instituted a search at John McVie's request, they could not be found. In 1996, however, the Dunecht Estate near Aberdeen decided to sell a set of eight bells cast in 1911 by the firm of Warners, Bellfounders of London. They had been hung in Dunecht House to celebrate the Coronation of George V. The Scottish Association of Change Ringers were anxious to keep the bells in Scotland, where there were only fourteen sets capable of being rung, and they managed to do so by raising £11,000 in interest free loans.

Remembering the story of St Mary's and its lost bells, the Association asked the church if it would like to purchase the Dunecht set. Although this would be an expensive operation, the Friends of St Mary's felt that it would be a fitting completion of all that had been done in past years, and they accepted. With a generous gift from Robin Salvesen and grants from the Scottish Association of Change Ringers itself and, through them, from the Manifold Trust, the Friends approached the National Heritage Lottery Fund for a contribution. The Fund at first agreed that the project was eligible, but then rejected the application. Deeply disappointed but unwilling to give up, the Appeals Committee urged the Fund to reconsider, and in the end, after much negotiation, St Mary's received a grant of £46,000.

One of the elders, Duncan Beaton, an experienced chartered civil engineer, agreed to act as project manager and Hayward Mills Associates, Bell Consultants and Contractors, Nottingham were employed to hang the bells. Removed from Dunecht in early December 1996, they had since been stored in Nottingham. They have a tenor of eleven and a quarter hundredweight in F#, and they were sent to Loughborough for some slight re-tuning before being brought to Haddington. Campbell and Smith of Ormiston began the necessary building work in the tower in early March, local volunteers helped the bellhangers, and the supporting fittings and frame were quickly built. On 19 April the bells, fittings and steel frame, weighing some twelve tons in all, were lifted into the tower by a crane with a 230 foot jib and the steel frame was fixed firmly in place with no fewer than between six and seven hundred bolts. Had there been the slightest movement in it, the vibration when the bells were rung would have caused dreadful damage to the church tower.

St Mary's had its bells again, but who was to ring them? An advertisement placed in the local paper evoked an enthusiastic response, and selected volunteers, ranging from eight-year-olds to retired people, began their training in March 1999. They were first of all given a demonstration at St Cuthbert's Church in Edinburgh, after which they were allowed to practice in the church at Stenton, a village near Haddington. Permitted to remove the clapper from its single bell, they held two hour training sessions three nights a week. On 30 April the Haddington Society of Change Ringers was inaugurated, with Nigel Booth and Dr Clare Caley as joint Ringing Masters and Alan Colley as Chairman.

The Right Rev. John Cairns, Moderator of the General Assembly of the Church of Scotland, dedicates the bells, 6 June 1999. (*Duncan Brash*)

The hanging of the bells and the adjustment of the fittings was completed and on 13 May 1999 the first test ring took place. Further practice followed, and on Sunday 6 June, the Right Reverend John Cairns, Moderator of the General Assembly of the Church of Scotland, dedicated the bells at a united service attended by the congregations of St Mary's and of Holy Trinity Church, Haddington. Ringers from as far away as Kent attended. The bells rang out softly both during and after the service and since then they have been rung for half an hour every Sunday morning. As Celia Hawkins, one of the ringers put it, 'The bells have drawn our community and congregations closer together and inspired many new friendships.' Just after noon on 1 January 2000, the bells of St Mary's were heard live on television when they featured as the first of thousands of British church bells in a special BBC programme for the new Millennium.

When the bells rang out, the congregation at St Mary's felt that their church had truly been made whole again and the long story of loss and reparation is nicely summed up by an incident which took place a few months later, at the beginning of May 2000. A concert in tribute to Yehudi Menuhin was being recorded in the church by the BBC, with Tamsin Little playing the Elgar Violin Concerto. In all the activity, someone managed to slip in and steal the small baptismal bowl with the inscription describing the re-opening of the church in 1812 after the earlier restoration. Although not of vast financial value, the bowl commemorated an important event in the history of St Mary's, and its loss was much regretted. Fortunately, the C.I.D. were able to arrest the person who had taken it, and they learned that the bowl had been thrown into the River Tyne. The police waded into the Tyne to search for it but, up to their chests in murky water, they were attacked by the local swans and forced to retreat. Everyone was deeply disappointed, but that very afternoon the bowl made a providential reappearance. A little girl found it by the Victoria Bridge, where it had been carried downstream by the current. She rescued it, took it to the police station, and it was returned to its rightful place in the church.

Conclusion

A SINGULAR SOLACE

No longer in part a romantic ruin, St Mary's stands complete, true to the intentions of the medieval masons who designed it more than six centuries ago. It is admired as a highly innovative architectural restoration and famous as a triumph of fundraising, but its real purpose remains unchanged. It is a building consecrated for spiritual purposes, where local people can worship God and mark some of the defining moments in their lives: baptism, marriage and death. Throughout the Middle Ages, priests celebrated Mass at the high altar beneath the east window, male choristers sang in Latin and the choir was the focal point of the church, the holiest part. Now there is no altar, both men, women and junior choristers sing in English and in other languages too, and the east window has long since lost its stained glass. So what have the minister and congregation done with their empty choir?

Ways of thinking about spirituality have undergone great change in the past thousand years, and not only in theology. In medieval times, the parishioners of St Mary's knelt to pray in a church glowing with colour and glittering with gold and silver reliquaries, cups and gilded statues. They also strolled about, chatted and laughed, stray dogs frolicking around their feet. After the Reformation, services were much more solemn affairs. No musical instruments were heard, the psalms were sung unaccompanied and people were expected to behave with dignity and decorum in an austere interior devoid of all ornament. Unpopular George Harley might raise a riot in 1805 by clambering over the pews to reach his desired seat, but the very fact that this incident went down in history is an indication of the horrified reaction of many of those present. That was not how people were supposed to behave in church.

During the Victorian era, soberly dressed families sat in their hard pews listening to very long sermons often twice a day on Sundays, and as late as the mid-twentieth century people went to church wearing their best clothes and speaking in reverential whispers. At the beginning of the twenty-first century, however, a greater informality once more prevails and the choir of St Mary's has become a place where this desire for a more relaxed atmosphere can be satisfied. The seats are arranged in the shape of a horseshoe so that everyone feels comfortable and conversation is encouraged. Soft toys lie on the thick carpet indicating that children are welcome and a short service is held there each Sunday morning. As one impressed visitor told the minister, the choir seemed to her to be like 'a womb, where little Christians are being conceived.' Light streams in through the plain leaded panes of the east

The east end of St Mary's arranged for a family service. *(Source unidentified)*

window, and people can clearly see the large copper beech tree which grows just outside, its seasonal changes a striking metaphor for life, death and renewal.

Throughout the year, conventional services are held in the nave each Sunday, with Communion on the second Sunday of the month in January, June and October, and sometimes also on the following Monday evening. The feasts of the Roman Catholic Church are no longer regarded as dates to be avoided, and there is Communion at both Christmas and Easter, with a Common Cup as well as individual glasses for the wine. An informal family Communion is held at the east end, with non-alcoholic wine in the Common Cup. Nor are longstanding traditions forgotten. Each February, the Friends of St Mary's organise a Candlemas Fair, and on that day the atmosphere in the church is strongly reminiscent of the Middle Ages. Trestle tables are put up in the choir and boxes of snowdrops and other plants are displayed there for sale, along with home baking, jam, marmalade, bottled fruit and books, while fiddlers and handbell ringers entertain the parishioners and visitors who sit and chat over tea, coffee, scones and cakes.

Reviving ancient traditions, the church has at the same time evolved to meet changing attitudes. Relations with other churches have developed and the Lauderdale Aisle has played a crucial part in this advance. Patrick, 17th Earl of Lauderdale, a devout Episcopalian, was for many years a Trustee of the famous Anglican shrine at Walsingham in Norfolk dedicated to the Virgin Mary. The shrine was restored in the 1950s by Father Hope-Patten, an Anglican priest, who used to say to the Earl, 'One day you must restore the shrine of Our Lady of Haddington' and in the late 1970s, thanks to the Earl's efforts, the Lauderdale Aisle was indeed restored, at first as a family chapel.

The chapel was re-consecrated in 1978 by Alistair Haggart, Episcopal Bishop of Edinburgh, and dedicated to the Virgin Mary, the Christ Child and the Three Kings. The Earl had commissioned from an Oberammergau wood carver living in Norfolk several figures representing the Three Kings paying homage to the Christ Child. These are displayed on the south wall, and there is an

An ecumenical gathering of clergy at St Mary's, with Patrick, Earl of Lauderdale in the centre, next to the Reverend Clifford Hughes. (*East Lothian Courier*)

icon from Mount Athos on the west wall, showing a similar scene. The table in the aisle is made from stones personally collected by the Earl from the Holy Land, Lourdes and other holy places. The re-consecration of the chapel was followed by an ecumenical service,. The Bishop of Edinburgh presided, the Very Reverend Dr Roy Sanderson, a former Moderator of the General Assembly of the Church of Scotland, took part, the Polish Orthodox priest in Edinburgh offered a prayer and the Roman Catholic Abbot of Nunraw blessed the carved figures. The chapel is available to every Trinitarian Church, be it for an Episcopalian Eucharist or a Roman Catholic Mass and members of the Presbyterian congregation of St Mary's meet there for a short prayer before their own Sunday morning service.

Even before he achieved the restoration of the Lauderdale Aisle, the Earl had instituted an annual pilgrimage to St Mary's. The first pilgrimage in 1970 attracted 13 pilgrims. By the year 2000 the number had risen to over a thousand. Those taking part visit St Mary's Church, Whitekirk, where a service is held in the morning. Mass is celebrated in St Mary's, Haddington at noon and, because of the large numbers of Roman Catholics attending, the Kirk Session give permission for this service to be held in the body of the church, something unthinkable for centuries after the Reformation. The climax to the pilgrimage follows in the afternoon, with an ecumenical service of healing. Clergy of all denominations go among the packed congregation to minister to anyone who raises a hand and asks for a prayer, giving to those seeking help a singular solace.

The service of healing in many ways symbolises what has happened in St Mary's. Old antagonists have been reconciled. The hostilities of Scots and English resulted in the ruin of the east end of the church, but Scots and English worked together to put it back as it had been. Presbyterians, Episcopalians and Roman Catholics, in the past divided by the most bitter enmities, now worship side by side at ecumenical services. Shared Christian convictions and a strong sense of community allowed the people of Haddington throughout the centuries to withstand invasion, fire, plague and flood. In our own time, they have been similarly inspired to achieve the seemingly impossible: the restoration of their great parish church.

SOURCES

In writing this book I have consulted a number of manuscript sources as well as printed books and articles. The records of the burgh of Haddington are kept in the National Archives of Scotland, Edinburgh under the category B30 and they have provided the information for the chapters on the history of the church, before the Reformation. They include charters and writs relating to St Mary's from as early as 1448, the burgh court books, which begin in 1555, and the minutes of council meetings from 1554 onwards. The earliest documents are printed in J.G.Wallace-Jones, *Charters and Writs concerning the Royal Burgh of Haddington* (Haddington, *c.*1895).

Dr J G. Wallace-Jones, who was a local historian, also made extracts from the Haddington burgh court books and common good accounts and his notes, which are in the National Archives of Scotland, GD1/413, are useful because they include passages from some early documents which no longer appear to be extant. Similarly, GD302/106 and 110 are modern handwritten references to passages in the burgh records mentioning St Mary's. All these later notes have been carefully made, and they would be useful for those who cannot read sixteenth-century handwriting. B.L.H.Horn, 'List of references to the pre-Reformation altarages in the parish church of Haddington' in *Transactions of the East Lothian Antiquarian and Field Naturalists' Society*, x, 55-91 provides a synopsis of the record evidence for the altars.

The progress of the siege of Haddington can best be studied in the letters of Lord Grey and others in *Calendar of the State Papers relating to Scotland and to Mary, Queen of Scots 1547-1603* ed. J. Bain and others (Edinburgh 1898-), volume i. Biographies of the leading figures of the period include Rosalind K. Marshall, *Mary of Guise* (London 1977 and, a concise version, Edinburgh 2001), Margaret H.B.Sanderson, *Cardinal of Scotland* [Cardinal Beaton] (Edinburgh 1986, new edn. 2001) and Rosalind K. Marshall, *John Knox* (Edinburgh 2000). Biographical information about the English commanders at the siege of Haddington is to be found in the *Dictionary of National Biography*, viii, 156, xv, 160 and xxi, 236. David J. Motherwell, 'The Siege of Haddington' in *East Lothian Life* (Autumn 1998, 20-21) provides a useful map of the siege.

For the post-Reformation era, the local presbytery records are also with the National Archives of Scotland. The most recent history of the town is *Haddington: Royal Burgh* (Phantassie 1997), an attractive, well-illustrated publication of 188 pages which may be supplemented by W. Forbes Gray and James H. Jamieson, *A Short History of Haddington* (1944; re-published, Stevenage 1986). This gives interesting detail. *Sinclair's Pictorial Guide to Haddington* (Haddington n.d.) includes John Richardson's 1881 recollections, with the story of George Harley, while Robert Gourlay and Anne Turner, *Historic Haddington* (Glasgow 1977), publishes the results of the modern official burgh survey. With the permission of the University of Glasgow (Department of Archaeology), Historic Scotland and Ordnance Survey, I am able to reproduce in this volume a map which was originally published in the burgh survey. It complements the text by illustrating the growth of the town and showing the course of the town wall. M. Lynch, M. Spearman and G. Stell, *The Scottish Medieval Town* (Edinburgh 1988) is valuable for comparative purposes.

As to the church itself, James Jamieson, *The Church of St Mary, Haddington* (Haddington 1949) is an excellent, if brief, account of the building's history and for visitors to the church there is a short, illustrated guidebook available. The *New Dictionary of National Biography* (2004) will contain an article on Patrick Cockburn, the first Protestant minister at St Mary's. Architectural details are to be found in Colin McWilliam, *Buildings of Scotland: Lothian except Edinburgh* (Edinburgh 1978) and *Royal Commission on the Ancient and Historical Monuments of Scotland: East Lothian* (1924), the standard works of reference.

For the story of the twentieth-century reconstruction, I have drawn heavily upon John McVie's privately published account, *The Restoration of St Mary's Parish Church, Haddington* (Haddington 1998), which describes the entire project from its inception. The Papers of Ian Lindsay & Partners, the architects, are deposited in the National Monuments Record, Edinburgh and provide vital, day by day details of the work of rebuilding, while the published Annual Reports and leaflets of the Lamp of Lothian record that Trust's aims and activities. I have also had the benefit of reading a description by Patrick, 17th Earl of Lauderdale of the development of the Lauderdale Aisle and the annual pilgrimage.

I received a number of informative papers and leaflets from the Reverend Clifford Hughes, relating to the church and to the Friends of St Mary's, and including an article by Celia Hawkins, 'Haddington: The Silence of the Bells' from *The Scottish Bell: the newsletter of the Scottish Association of Change Ringers*, 7 (1999) along with a report on the bells published in *The Ringing World: the weekly journal for church bell ringers* 4603 (16 July 1999). I have also benefited greatly from information received from those whom I have thanked in the acknowledgements.

AUTHOR'S ACKNOWLEDGEMENTS

This is an account of how the Parish Church of St Mary's, Haddington was built, partially destroyed and, after more than four hundred years, restored again in a manner which has seemed to many to be little short of miraculous. John McVie, solicitor and former Town Clerk of Haddington, was the moving spirit behind the reconstruction, which he energetically drove through despite strong opposition and complicated bureaucracy. In 1998 he produced his own recollections of the events of the 1960s and 70s, and this proved so fascinating that the Minister and Congregational Board of St Mary's decided that they would like to publish a more general account for a wider public. I was delighted to be invited to write this book, for I well remember gazing at the ruined east end of St Mary's, never imagining that I would see it with its chancel, tower and transepts restored. My later chapters have drawn extensively on John's account and I owe him my special thanks. The present text would not have been written without him.

A number of other people have also given me their generous assistance. The Minister, the Reverend Clifford Hughes, has been a constant source of encouragement and has supplied me with much valuable information, particularly about the church as it is today. Her Grace Elizabeth, Duchess of Hamilton, who played such a vital part in making the restoration possible, very kindly spoke to me about the founding of The Lamp of Lothian and presented me with copies of all the Lamp's Annual Reports and the relevant leaflets. Duncan Brash, whose dramatic photographs record the restoration, willingly supplied many of the illustrations and kindly took various new pictures, including the view of the church on the cover. John Reid drew my attention to the papers of Ian Lindsay & Partners, architects for the project, Crichton Lang spoke eloquently of the moving atmosphere in the church during the work, Robin Salvesen told me about the repairs of the 1980s and Duncan Beaton explained in detail how the bells were installed. Veronica Steele of the National Monuments Record has been indefatigable in her assistance, and the Very Reverend Dr Duncan Shaw gave me his valuable comments on my chapter about the medieval church. Finally I am most grateful to all the owners of the paintings and photographs reproduced in this book.

R.K.M.
21 October 2000

INDEX

The numbers in *italics* refer to illustrations

Aberdeen 63
Aberlady 7, 20, 26, 28
Aitchison, Helen 34
Aitchison, Jane 34
Aitchison, Margaret 34
Albany, John Stewart, Duke of 10
Alderston 34
Alexander II, King of Scots 7
Allan, Maxwell, artist 51
Amos, George 34
Ancient Monuments Board 40
Anderson, John, chaplain 23
Angus 13
Annand, James, Session Clerk, St Mary's 38
Argyll, Archibald Campbell, 4th Earl of 14
Arran, James Hamilton, 2nd Earl of *see* Châtelherault, Duke of
Athos, Mount 67
Audan, Wystan Hugh, poet 46
Ayton, John, Provost of Haddington 25
Aytoun, William, glazier 25

Bach, Johann Sebastian, composer 62
Badenoch, Sir Cameron 39, 43
Bakers' Trade Incorporation 11, 22, 29, 31
'The Ballad of Barnaby' 46
Ballantine, Alexander, stained glass artist 34
Bank of Scotland 52
Baring's Bank 39
Barnet & Morton, Messrs 51
Barns 28
Barns, Janet 22
Barns, John 22
Barns, Margaret 22
BBC (British Broadcasting Corporation) 62, 64
Beaton, Cardinal David, Archbishop of St Andrews 5, 8, 13
Beaton, Duncan, civil engineer 63
Berwick-upon-Tweed 6, 7, 14, 16
Berwickshire 24
Bible, the 12, 25, 62
  Exodus, Book of 32
  Psalms, Book of 24, 34
  Psalms, metrical 25
Blackburn Cathedral 56
Blantyre, Alexander Stewart, 5th Lord 12
Board of Works 34
Bolton 25
Bolton Church 42
Booth, Nigel, Ringing Master 63
Border Abbeys 16
Border, the 14
Borders, the 7, 19, 21
Borthwick, Patrick, goldsmith 26, 31, 52
Bothwell, Patrick Hepburn, 3rd Earl of 13
Bowes, Sir Robert 16
Bradford 47
Brash, Duncan, Session Clerk, St Mary's 58
Brende, John, muster master 16
Brennan, Archibald, tapestry designer 59
Brinton, Thomas, Bishop of Exeter 9
British Linen Bank 37, 48
Broun of Colstoun family 27
Burghers and Anti-Burghers 27
Burne-Jones, Sir Edward 47, 56
Burns, Gilbert, factor 32
Burns, Ian, surveyor 37-8
Burns, Robert, poet 32
Bute, John Stuart, 6th Marquis of 52

Cairns, John, 58
Cairns, The Right Reverend John 64, ***64***
Caley, Dr Clare, Ringing Master 63
Calvin, John, theologian 25
Campbell, Colin 60
Campbell, Henry, mason 25-6
Campbell, John, glazier 25
Campbell, Mungo 52
Campbell & Smith (Construction) Co. Ltd. 61, 63
Canada 36, 62
Candlemas Fair 66
Cargill 33
Carlyle, Thomas, historian 32-3, 35
Carlyle, Mrs Jane Welsh 32-3, 35
Carmichael, The Reverend James, Minister of St Mary's 25
Carmondean 34
Carnegie Trust UK 43
Carpenter, Richard, of Harpendene 10-11
CDW, glaziers 50
Chalmers, The Reverend Thomas, founder of the Free Church of Scotland 27
Charles I, King 27
Charles II, King 27-8
Châtelherault, James Hamilton, 2nd Earl of Arran, Duke of 5-6, 14, 16, 18-19, 21, ***21***
Choicelee 24
Christian Stewardship Campaign 39
Christie, John, of Cowden 34, 38
Church & Co, organ builders 62
Church of Scotland 27, 42, 45
  Advisory Committee on Artistic Questions 46
  Disruption of the 27
  General Assembly 27
  General Trustees 39-40, 43, 47, 60
  General Trustees Ecclesiastical Buildings Committee 39, 46
  Presbytery of Haddington and Dunbar 39, 43
CID (Criminal Investigation Department) 64
Clerkington 16
Cockburn, Daniel, wright 28
Cockburn, James 25
Cockburn, James, wright 28
Cockburn, Janet *see* Kemp, Mrs Janet
Cockburn, Laurence, wright 28
Cockburn, The Reverend Patrick, Minister of St Mary's 24-5
Cockburn, William 11
Collegiate status 8

INDEX

Colley, Alan, Chairman of Haddington Society of Change Ringers 63
Cologne Cathedral 10
Colstoun 27, 36
Commissioners of Works 32
Communion 9, 12, 25, 31-2, 57, 59, 66
Compostella, St James's Shrine 10
Cook, The Reverend Dr John, Minister of St Mary's 33
Council for the Care of Churches 47
Coventry Cathedral 38
Cowden 34
Croft, Sir James 20
Crossar, John, chaplain 22

Dalkeith Castle 16
David I, King of Scots 7
David, King (Biblical) 34
Davidson, The Very Reverend Nevile, Dr 47, 51-2, 58
Davidson, Mrs Margaret 58
Davie, Jimmy, plumber 60
Denholm, James 45
Dickson, Hester, pianist 46
Dickson, Joan, cellist 46
Dodds, Robert, mason 26
Donaldson, James, sculptor 34
Douglas, John 25
Dovecote Tapestry Studios 59
Dryburgh Abbey 5
Drysdale, Mrs H D 34
Duke University, North Carolina 62
Dumbarton 19
Dumfriesshire 33-4, 47
Dunbar 16, 18
Dunbar Castle 20
Dunbar Collegiate Church 24
Dunecht Estate 63
Dunecht House 63
Duns 50
Durham 47
  Cathedral 63
  Dean of 63

East Lothian 7, 12, 14, 42, 46, 59
  Antiquarian and Field Naturalists Society 36, 43
  County Council 52
  County Council Planning Authority 40, 47
  County Planning Officer *see* Tindall, Frank
Edinburgh 5, 7, 13-14, 19, 21-2, 24-7, 34, 36-7, 39-40, 49, 51, 54-5, 57, 59, 66-7
  Caledonian Station 49
  Castle 5, 23
  Chancelot Flour Mills 49
  Duke of *see* Philip, HRH Prince
  Holyrood, Abbey of 5, 16
  St Cecilia's Hall 61
  St Cuthbert's Church 34, 55, 63
  St Giles Church (later Cathedral) 8, 27, 55
  St James's Square 49
  St Paul's Episcopal Church (later St Paul's and St George's) 31
  Tolbooth 28
  Treaty of 23
  Trinity College Church 28
  University 33, 62
  York Place 31
Edward III, King of England 7
Edward VI, King of England 5-6, 21
Elgar, Sir Edward, composer 64
Elizabeth I, Queen of England 22
Elizabeth II, Queen 58, ***58***
Elizabeth, Queen, The Queen Mother 46, 61
Elliot, Archibald, architect 31
EMI Recording Studio 44
England 5, 12, 14, 25, 56
Episcopal Church of Scotland 45
Esk Burn 6
d'Essé, André de Montalembert, Sieur 16, 19
European Architectural Heritage Award 60
Everest, Mount 42
Exeter 9

Fairbairn, James, master mason 59
Faunt, Harry, fruiterer 36
Ferguson, Bill 58
Fife 5
First Book of Discipline 27
Flanders 11
Fleming, Lady Jane *see* Maitland, Lady Jane
Fleming, Tom, actor 46
Fleshers' Trade Incorporation 31
Forman, The Reverend James, Minister of St Mary's 27
Formasons, stone cleaners 55
Forres, George 19
Forrest, John 21
Forth, River 5, 7, 19
Foster & Andrews, organ builders 34
'Four Maries, The' (ballad) 46
France 5-6, 16, 18-19, 24
François, Dauphin of France, later François II 18-19, 24
Fraser, Thomas, mason 31
Free Church of Scotland 27
Furde, John of 11
Furriers' Trade Incorporation 11

Galashiels, Langside Church 56
Garvald 8, 33-4, 47
General Assembly *see* Church of Scotland
Geneva 25
George V, King 63
Germany 12, 62
Giffordgate *see* Haddington
Graham, Peter, and Partners, quantity surveyors 45, 48
Gray, John, carter 26
Greenwich, Treaties of 5
Grey of Wilton, William, 13th Lord 6, 14, 16
Grier, George, minister 29
Grier, Mrs George 29
Grimsby 47

Haddington 5-7, 10, 12, 13, 14, 16, 18, 20-3, 25-6, 31-2, 34, 36-7, 39, 42-3, 58, 60, 63, 67
  Abbey Bastion 16
  Bridge Youth Centre 43
  Burgh crest 8, 59-60

Cistercian Nunnery 7, 14, 19
Dean of Guild Court 47-8
Franciscan Friary 7, 18, 20, 26, 42
Giffordgate 13
Governor of *see* Wilford, Sir James
Haddington House 36, 42-3, 48, 58, 60
Hardgate 7, 16
High Street 7, 16
Holy Trinity Church 64
John of 10
Knox Academy 46
Lady Kitty's Garden 37
Magistrates 28, 31
Market cross 7, 29
Market Street 7, 10, 16
Newton Port 36, 51
Nungate 16-17
Nungate Bridge 7, 28
Plan ***17***, ***29***
Poldrate Mill and Granary 42-4, 54
St Martin's Church 29
St Mary's Church *see* St Mary's Church, Haddington
Secession Church, Anti-Burgher 32
Sidegate 7, 10
Siege of 13-22, 25, 35, 42
Society of Change Ringers 63
Tiberio's Bastion 16
Tolbooth 6-7, 14, 16, 18, 25, 28
Tolbooth Street 22
Tolbooth Wynd 7
Town Council 7-8, 11, 22-5, 27, 43, 60
Town House 39
Treasurer of 22-3, 26
Treaty of 19
Victoria Bridge 61
Haddingtonshire Courier 38
Haddow, T Harley & Partners, structural engineers 45-6, 49, 61
Haggart, Alistair, Bishop of Edinburgh 66-7
Hall, Alexander and Son, builders 49-50, 54, 57
Hamilton, Douglas Douglas-Hamilton, 14th Duke of 42, 44, 55, 57-8
Hamilton, Lady Elizabeth Percy, Duchess of 42-5, 48, 51-3, ***54***, 55, 57-9
Hamilton Palace 42
Hammermen's Trade Incorporation 29
Harley, George, copper and tin smith 31, ***31***, 65
Harpendene 10
Harris, The Reverend John, Assistant Minister of St Mary's 47
Hastie, George, mason 26
Hawkins, Celia, bell-ringer 64
Hay, George, architect 47
Hay, John, of Aberlady 28
Hayward Mills Associates, bell consultants and contractors 63
Henderson, Joe, beadle, St Mary's 58
Henri II, King of France 6, 18-19
Henry III, King of England 7
Henry VIII, King of England 5, 12, 14
Henshaw, Charles & Sons Ltd, architectural metalworkers 55
Herdmanston 14
Hertford, Earl of *see* Somerset, Duke of
Historic Buildings Council 61
Holcroft, Sir Thomas 18
Holy Land 67
Hooker, Craigmyle, Scotland Ltd, fund-raisers 53
Hope-Patten, Father 66
House-of-Muir 31
Howden, Agnes 33
Howden, Dr Thomas, senior 33
Howden, Dr Thomas, junior 33
Hughes, The Reverend Clifford, Minister of St Mary's 3, 62-3, ***63***, ***66***
Hull 34
Huntingdon, Ada, Countess of 7

Ingaldistoun, Robert of 10
Iona 59
Iona Abbey 40

James III, King of Scots 10
James III, children of 10
James V, King of Scots 5, 10, 12, 18, 22
James VI, King of Scots 25, 27
Jedburgh Abbey 5
JL Floor Finishing Company Ltd 60
John, King of England 7

Kello, Tom of 10
Kemp, William 10-11
Kemp, Mrs Janet, 10-11
Kennedy, Catherine, Lady 44
Kennedy, General Sir John 44
Kent 6, 16, 64
Kilmaine, John Browne, 6th Lord 40
Kirkcaldy 51
Knox, James, sculptor 34
Knox, John, Reformer 13, ***13***, 22, 24, 27
Kylesmuir 28

Laminators (Lowestoft) Limited, boat builders 47, 54-5, ***55***
Lammermuir Pipe Organs 62-3
'Lamp of Licht, The' 46, 54
Lamp of Lothian, The 7, 42-6, 48, 57, 60
Collegiate Centre 43, 46
Collegiate Trust 42-45, 48, 52, 60
Trustees 42-4
Lanarkshire 42
Lang, Crichton, architect 49-51, 54-5, 57, 60-1
Lauder 28
Lauderdale, Earls of 47
Lauderdale, John Maitland, 1st Duke of 28, 42
Lauderdale, Patrick Maitland, 17th Earl of ***66***, 66-7
Lawson, John 10
Lawson, Marion 10
Leith 5, 16, 19, 22, 25
South Leith Parish Church 28
Leith Glazing 50
Lennoxlove (Lethington Tower) 13, 16, 27-8, 32, 42-4
Leonard and Partners, engineers 39
Lethington Tower *see* Lennoxlove
Levine, Rhoda, choreographer 46

INDEX

Liddiard & Burns, RVM, chartered surveyors 38-9
Lindsay, Lady Broun, of Colstoun 36, 42
Lindsay, Ian G, architect 40
Lindsay, Ian G and Partners, architects 41, 43, 45
Linlithgow 37, 57
  St Michael's Church 36, ***36***, 38, 44
Little, Tamsin, violinist 64
Liverpool Cathedral 56
Locharbriggs Quarries, Dumfries 33, 47
London 14, 33, 40, 44, 48, 55, 62-3
  Airport 44
  Victoria and Albert Museum 47
Lords of the Congregation 22, 24
Lorimer, The Reverend Dr Robert, Minister of St Mary's 32
Lothian 5, 13
Loughborough 63
Lourdes 67
Lowestoft 47
Luther, Martin, Reformer 12
Lyall, Andrew 25

Macdonell, The Reverend Alastair, Minister of St Mary's 61
MacGregor, The Reverend Dr James 34
MacPhail, Stewart 41, 58
McRobbie, Alec 58
McVie, John, solicitor, town clerk of Haddington 35-8, 40-5, 48-9, 51, ***51***, 55, 57, ***58***, 58-9, 60, 63
McVie, Mrs Lindsaye 37, 55, 58
Maitland, Isabella, Lady, wife of John, 1st Lord Maitland 27-8
Maitland, Jane, Lady, wife of John, 2nd Lord Maitland 27-8
Maitland, John, 1st Lord 27-8
Maitland, John, 2nd Lord 27-8
Maitland of Lethington, Sir Richard 13
Maitland, Robert 21
Malcolm, Alec, bank manager 37-8, 45
Maltmen's Trade Incorporation 11
Manchester 62
Manifold Trust 63
Margaret of Denmark, Queen of Scots 10
Mary I, Queen of England 21-2
Mary of Guise, Queen of Scots 5-6, 14, 16, ***18***, 18-19, 21-3
Mary, Queen of Scots 5, 18-19, 24-5
Masons' Trade Incorporation 11-12, 29
Mass 8-12, 23-4, 65, 67
Mauchlin, James, chaplain 11, 23
Mauchlin, Patrick 11
Mauchlin, Thomas 11, 22
Melrose Abbey 5
Menuhin, Hepzibah, concert pianist 54, ***54***
Menuhin, Yehudi, violinist 44-5, 54, ***54***, 60, 64
Millar, Mungo, chaplain 12
Miller, David 58
Milligan, Christine 61
Mills, Derick, Session Clerk, St Mary's 40, 44-5, 58
Milne, Lennox, actress 46
Minay, William, organist 55-6
Ministry of Works 34-43, 47
Moat sandstone 34
Moncrieff, Alec, Messrs, builders 39-40
Moray, James, Earl of *see* Stewart, Lord James
Morton, James Douglas, 4th Earl of 25

Munro, John 40
Murray, Marion *see* Stirling, Mrs Marion
Musselburgh 5-6, 16

National Covenant 27
National Heritage Lottery Fund 63
Natural Stone Quarries, Durham 47, 50, 52-3
Nimmo Smith, Austin 33
Nimmo Smith, Frances 33
Nimmo Smith, Hilda 33, 35-7, 38-9, 45, 51, ***51***, 57-8, ***58***
Nimmo Smith, Mrs Jean, first wife of Dr Robert Nimmo Smith 33
Nimmo Smith, Mabel 33
Nimmo Smith, (Mary) Dorothea 33
Nimmo Smith, Mrs Mary Anne, second wife of Dr Robert Nimmo Smith 33
Nimmo Smith, The Reverend Dr Robert, Minister of St Mary's 33-4, 36-7
Nimmo Smith, Robert, junior 33
Norfolk 66
North Carolina 62
Northumberland 62
Northumberland, Alan Percy, 8th Duke of 42
Nottingham 63
Nunraw, Abbot of 67
Nunraw, Abbey of 46, 67

Oberammergau 66
Oldhamstocks 62
Old Lights and New Lights 27
Oliphant, James 22, 24
Ormiston 13-14, 31, 61, 63
Ormiston, Peter, builder 33
'Our Lady's Juggler' 46

Paisley, John Hamilton, Abbot of 5
Palmer, Sir Thomas 16, 18-19
Paris 24
  University of (Sorbonne) 24
  Professor of Oriental Languages 24
Parkinson-Twaddle, JTL, Ltd, heating engineers 53-4, 60
Parry, Sir Hubert, composer 62
Paterson, (John) Wilson, architect 37-41, 46
Percy, Lady Elizabeth *see* Hamilton, Duchess of
Perth 14, 22
Philip, Prince, Duke of Edinburgh 58
Pilgrim Trust 39, 40, 48-9
Pilgrimages, 10, 67
Pinkie, Battle of 6, 16
Polish Orthodox priest 67
Porter, John, bank manager 48, 58
Presbytery of Haddington and Dunbar *see* Church of Scotland
Preston 5
Privy Council, Scottish 28
Proudfoot, The Reverend William, Minister of St Mary's 34
Psalms *see* Bible
Punton, Thomas 27

Reformation 24, 26-7, 65, 67
Reformation Parliament 23, 25
Reiach, Alan, architect 36, 38

Reid, John, architect 41, 44, 47, 49, 51, 57, 59
Rentokil 45
Research for Truth Foundation 52
Rhind, John, sculptor 34
Rhind, W Birnie, sculptor 34
Riach, The Reverend James, Minister of St Mary's 48, 51, **51**, 58-9
Riach, Mrs Elizabeth 58
Richenton, John 19
Richerby, Neil, organ builder 62
Richmond and Lennox, Frances, Duchess of 42
Robertson, Duncan 58
Robertson, Duncan, tenor 46
Roman Catholic Church 12, 18, 23-5, 45, 66
Ross, Robert, Bishop of 10
Royal Air Force 42
Royal Fine Art Commission 41, 47
Royal Northern College of Music 62
Royal Scots, 1st Battalion 60
Rusack, Dr Louis 51, 55-6, 58, 62
Rushworth & Dreaper Ltd, organ builders 47
Rutherford, Alexander, mason 31
Rutland, Henry Manners, 2nd Earl of, Warden of the East and Middle Marches 20

St Andrew 10-11
St Andrews 5, 8, 13, 22
  Castle 13
  Diocese of 17
  Grammar School 25
  Prior of 7, 22
  Priory of Augustinian Canons 7, 22, 24
  St Andrews University 13, 24
St Anne 10-11
St Aubert 10-11, 22
St Bartholomew 10
St Bees stone 17, 50
St Blaise *see* St Eloi
St Catherine the Virgin 10
St Columba 59
St Crispian 10-11
St Crispin 10-11
St Doicho (?Duthac) 10-11
St Duthac 12
St Eloi (Blaise) 10-11
St James the Great 10-11, 23
St John the Baptist 10-12
St John the Divine 34
St John the Evangelist 10-11
St Mary *see* Virgin Mary, The
St Mary's Church, Haddington
  Altars 7-12, 22-27, 65
  Appeals Committee 63
  Baptismal bowl 32, 64
  Bell-ringers 11, 63
  Bells 8, 9, 20, 25, 36, 39, 57, 62-4
  Budgeting Committee 60
  Candlesticks 32
  Chalices 9, 11, 22
  Chancel 7 *see* also choir
  Choristers 8, 11, 65
  Church Hall 36
  Churchyard 7-8, 19, 25-6
  Columba Aisle 59
  Columba Chapel 59
  Communion cups 26, **26**, 31, 52, 55, 66
  Communion tables 34, 60
  Congregational Board 60
  Consecration cross ***8***
  Council of Friends of St Mary's 60
  Fabric Committee 60
  Fabric Fund 61
  Font 34
  Friends of St Mary's 45, 48, 52, 54, 57, 60, 63, 66
  Guardians of St Mary's 60
  Joint Financial Co-ordinating Committee 48
  Kirk Session 26, 36, 38-45, 47-8, 52-3, 57, 67
  Lady Aisle 59
  Lady Chapel *see* Lady Aisle
  Lauderdale Aisle 32, 47, 66-7
  Lauderdale Monument ***29***
  Lauderdale Vault 28, 35, 47
  Lectern 34
  Lofts 27-34
  Nimmo Smith Memorial Committee 41
  Organ Committee 55-6
  Organs 25, 34, 37, 39, 47-8, ***50***, 50-1, 55-6, ***62***, 62-3
  Paintings 25
  Patens (plates) 11, 27, 31
  Pews 32, 58-9
  Pilgrim badge ***10***
  Pillar of repentance 26
  Plan ***33***
  Plates *see* patens
  Promotion and Management Committee 61
  Pulpits 8, 25-6, 31-2, 34, 61
  Reredos 8
  Restoration Committee 38, 40, 42, 47-8, 51, 57-9, 61
  Rood screen 8-9
  Session House 39
  Statues 25
  Tapestries 59
  Vestments 11, 25, 27
  Wemyss Memorial Window 33, 56, **56**, 58-9
  Windows 8, 21, 25, 32-4, 39-40, 47, 50, 53, 55-6, 61, 65-6

St Michael the Archangel 10-11
St Nicholas 10
St Ninian 10
St Peter 10-11
St Salvator 10, 22, 27
St Severus 10
St Thomas 10

Saltoun Hall 14
Salvesen, Robin, Chairman of St Mary's Congregational Board 61, 63
Sanderson, The Very Reverend Dr Roy 67
Scene in an Old Gothic Church, A 31, ***31***
Scheyle, James 11
Scotland 5-6, 8, 12-14, 18-20, 22-3, 27-8, 56, 60, 63
Scotsman newspaper 37, 57
Scottish Association of Change Ringers 63
Scottish Development Department 41, 43

INDEX

Scottish Office 60
Scottish Post Office Board 62
Secretary of State for Scotland 40, 48
Seggarsdean 8
Seton, George, of Barns 28
Seton, Lady Isabella *see* Maitland, Lady Isabella
Seton Palace 5
Seton, William, Provost of Haddington 28
Seton, Sir William, of Kylesmuir 28-9
Shearer, Mr, foreman, Alexander Hall and Son 57
Shoemakers' Trade Incorporation 11
Shrewbury, Francis Talbot, 5th Earl of 19
Sibbald, The Reverend Dr William, Minister of St Mary's 32
Simpson, Alexander 21
Simpson, Andrew 25
Sinclair of Stevenson family 27
'Singular Solace' 54
Skinners' Trade Incorporation 11
Smith, Bill 58
Smith, William Allan and Company Ltd, electrical contractors 54
Smiths' Trade Incorporation 11, 31
Society of Friends 45
Solway Moss, Battle of 5
Somerset 47
Somerset, Edward Seymour, Earl of Hertford, Duke of 5-6, 14, 16, 18-19, 21
Sorbonne *see* Paris, University of
Sotheby's, auctioneers 55
Spain 10
Spowage, Fraser, Provost of Haddington 51, ***51***, 58
Spowage, Mrs Isabelle 58
Stanley, John, composer 62
Steele, The Very Reverend Dr David Steel 44
Stenton 63
Stevenson 27
Stevenson, John, glazier 25
Stewart, Lord James, Prior of St Andrews, later Earl of Moray 22, **23**, 24, 27
Stewart, W, organist 34
Stirling, John, solicitor 34
Stirling, Mrs Marion 34
Stoddart, William, hammerman 29
Switzerland 43

Tailors' Trade Incorporation 11
Tait, John, chaplain 12
Templedean 34
Tenterfield 34
Thirlestane Castle 28
Thomson, Bernard 22, 24-5
Thomson, The Reverend James, Minister of St Mary's 35, 38, 43, 47
Thow, James, glazier 50
'Three Ballads' 46
Three Kings (of Cologne), The 10, 23, 66
Tiberio 16
Tindall, Frank, County Planning Officer, East Lothian 41, 47, 60
Tod, Mary Anne *see* Nimmo Smith, Mary Anne
Torquay, St Michael's Church 47, 55
Trades Incorporations 11, 29, 31
Trinity, The 10-11
'True Thomas' 46
Tunbridge Wells 28
Turner, Charles, composer 46
Tweed, River 5
Tyne, River 7, 35, 64

Vallance, John 29
Virgin Mary, The 7-13, 24, 26-7, 65-6

Walker, J W, organ builders 56, 62
Walsingham 66
Wandestoun, Robert 11
Warburton, William, mason 31
Warners, bellfounders 63
Watson and Ryman Ltd, office supplies 55
Weavers' Trade Incorporation 31
Welsh, Dr John 35
Wemyss and March, Francis David Charteris, 12th Earl of 36, 42, 45, 56, 58
Wemyss and March, Francis Charteris, 9th Earl of 33
Wemyss and March, Francis Charteris, 10th Earl of 33
Wesley, Samuel Sebastian, composer 62
Whitehaven paving 53
Whitekirk, St Mary's Church 67
Wilford, Sir James 14, ***15***, 16, 19-20
William I (William the Lion), King of Scots 7
Williams, Professor Peter 62
Wilson, Adam 22
Wilson, Martin 22
Wilson, William, burgh and parish clerk of Haddington 23
Wilson, William, glass stainer 34
Winning, Cardinal Thomas ***63***
Wishart, George 12-13, ***14***
Wood, Tommy 58-60
Wren, James 61
Wrights' Trade Incorporation 11-12, 29
Wyndham, Captain 16, 18

Yester House 14
York 20
  Minster 56

Zwingli, Ulrich, theologian 25